id rather
be *seen*
than
viewed

I'd rather
be *seen*
than
viewed

columns by

JANE FISHMAN

SAVANNAH, GEORGIA

ISBN 978 0 578 86997 1

Cover Illustration by Melinda Borysevicz

Book design by Ariel Janzen

Edited by Eugene Downs

For additional copies, visit your local bookstore or Amazon.com.

for CARMELA

CONTENTS

*The trick is
growing up
without
growing old.*

—

CASEY STENGEL

INTRODUCTION

"I loved that column about Alexa," a good friend told me after I said I was collecting some of my favorites for a book (only he said Siri, by mistake). "The time you asked her, 'When am I going to die?'"

"Not sure I remember that one, Dan," I said, "but it sounds like something I'd try to sneak in, especially during Covid times." Twenty years after publishing my first collection, *Everyone's Gotta Be Somewhere*, and thirty years after I started writing columns for the Savannah Morning News, I'm still looking for answers, still trying to figure out what connects us, still trying to figure out what it's all about. Is it food? Butterflies? Birthdays? Astrological signs?

"Nice to see you," people like to say in Savannah, even if we hardly know one another.

"Better to be seen than viewed," I quip, leaving it at that. Gallows humor, I suppose. It appeals to me.

So do lists.

In *twenty* years, I've had:

ten chickens,	*nine* passwords,
eight upgrades,	*seven* dentists,
six dogs,	*five* computers,
four street addresses,	*three* cell phones,
two phone numbers,	*one* partner.

I got the list habit from my mother. She kept a spiral notebook with a summary page for each month of the year. This is one of my favorites; it includes all the major categories of life:

April 1989:
Michelle's bar mitzvah;
lunch with Harry, Maggie, Ana;

root canal;
Dorothy found tumor on colon;
tripped at Original Pancake;
Lucille Ball died.

Between the first book and this one, some things have changed, some haven't. The headline from one of the columns in this book—"Savannah: I love you; I don't always like you"—says a lot.

One thing about Savannah and my place in it has stayed the same: the excuse to talk to people and a column around which to organize my thoughts. This is what motivates me to write. In a town this size, there's a certain trust. The other day I went to buy a political sign from folk artist Scott Stanton (aka, Panhandle Slim). He had set up in the parking lot of Lucky's Market, which had gone belly up earlier this year, before the pandemic. I got there early, knowing how popular his signs and T-shirts are.

Scott likes to keep things simple. No Venmo for him. No chip for credit cards. No price on the signs. Pay what you want, he says. When a young woman showed up with no cash, my girlfriend said to her, "Venmo money to me." Then I—who, like Panhandle, can't be bothered with Venmo—could hand over cash to him because I never leave home without it. Then she would buy me dinner.

In some ways, two decades later, it's an easier environment to smoke out stuff about folks. You Google them. That was not available twenty years ago. You could talk directly to them. Talking one-to-one is a far better way to connect. People answered their phones. That's how I reached James Alan McPherson, the first African-American to win the Pulitzer Prize for Fiction—and a graduate of Savannah's Beach High School. I got his number from the "long distance operator," dialed him up and reached him in his office at the Iowa Writers' Workshop. It was a reluctant interview. McPherson, a fine writer, is not a braggart. He was soft-spoken, modest and in Iowa, a long way away from his Savannah birthplace.

On the other hand, connection opportunities abound. Just the other morning, as I drank the day's first cup of coffee, I stood near my favorite 8-year-old as she talked on Messenger Kids to a 9-year-old friend in Tokyo. They carried on as if they were blocks apart.

A few weeks before that, I got to harvest heirloom rice at Wormsloe State Historic Site. I wouldn't have known anything about that twenty years ago. With the inimitable researcher Sarah Ross orchestrating and rice grower and horticulturist Rollen Chalmers leading the way, we stood in the marshy water canals (trying to avoid copperheads) and wielded sharp instruments to snap off the long panicles or clusters, which we jammed into a large, black plastic bag. Later, Rollen—a member of the fourth generation in his family to grow rice—would take it to a mill in South Carolina to be threshed. The origins of this Carolina Gold rice go back to the 1760s. Ross directs the University of Georgia Center for Research and Education. In her search for heirloom seeds, she farms plots on the Barrow family's private property at Wormsloe. Last year, among other things, she grew forty-two kinds of okra and thirty-seven varieties of collards.

Over the years, when I couldn't find anything to write about in Savannah, I'd get the heck out of town. I'd put my eyes on something else, listen to a different accent, feel a different part of the country. I used to drive, but then I switched to the train. It didn't really matter where it was going. Many of those observations made it into my last book, *So What's the Hurry? Tales from the Train.* A few people who don't like to travel thanked me for the book. It meant they didn't have to get on a train. They could travel through my eyes. Glad to oblige, I say. Happy to help.

I've learned a few tricks about living along the way.

> Cut your losses.
> Don't look in the mirror too much.
> Keep lentils in the house.
> Can't remember a name? Go through the alphabet. It starts with an 'S'.

I've learned to rely on old columns, too. They can be random, they can be arbitrary, hanging by a thread. They are my kind of spiral notebook. They help me remember people, moments, hurricanes, adventures, catastrophes, mishaps and epiphanies. Maybe they'll do the same for you.

Enjoy.

" *Sign at the entrance of Hyde Park in London:* DO NOT ALLOW YOUR DOG TO CHASE, WORRY, OR INJURE WILDLIFE."

RANDOM RAMBLINGS

1 / *You look like you own some cotton in Augusta (Speaking of drag queens and such)*

Is it too late to be grateful? With all the turkey and such from Thanksgiving long-consumed, long digested, long gone (or long forgotten in the rear of the refrigerator), I forget if I stopped to remember all the good things. Or question why we associate gratitude with Thanksgiving in the first place. Sometimes the only quiet times conducive to contemplation are spent reading poetry (try it, you might like it), drinking a cup of coffee away from the computer or a book, sitting outside (in December, in flip-flops) watching the cardinals, watching the leaves fall as if they were snowflakes, noticing a fence of purple morning glories still thriving (in December). So much fall color this year. Have you noticed? It's an anomaly, a deviation, for sure. I like it.

Speaking of deviations, I am grateful to people who make us think. Like Trevor Noah.

"It's always curious to me when white people shake their heads, look all serious and compassionate and say, 'I can't imagine what it's like for you out in the world, as a Black man and all, all you have to put up with,'" said Noah. "That's when I pause, look them in the eyes and say, 'Try. Try to imagine.'"

Or Michael Eric Dyson, who just wrote *JAY-Z: Made in America*, castigating the term "Black on Black" crime. Dyson says, "No one ever talks about 'White on White' crime, which is how most crime

3

among White people occurs."

I am grateful to people of a certain age who grew up when language was more florid, more metaphorical, more appreciated, people who knew the value of apostrophes, an endangered species, who don't overuse exclamation points, an area to which I find myself drifting dangerously close.

"You look like you own some cotton in Augusta," Virginia, a 93-year-old, said to me the other day.

"Wha'?" I said. "What in the heck does that mean?"

"It means you are top drawer," she said without missing a beat. "The bee's knees. The cat's meow." I'll take it.

"Pancakes: So good it don't need syrup," boasts a wall on Narobia's Grits & Gravy, a café on Habersham Street in Savannah. I doubt you'd hear that from Virginia. The verb and subject don't match. She's big on verbs and subjects matching. Still, I kind of like it.

How about the name "Elvis"? For a woman? That's a new one on me. I like that too.

I'm grateful to hear the word "harvest" used for something other than bringing in the crops. This usage, thanks in no small part to spooky 21st-century operations such as the now-defunct Cambridge Analytica (can you say Big Brother?), an outfit that put themselves on the map every day, every hour for "harvesting data." That would be information about you and me.

Which reminds me of something a smart friend of mine savvy to the ways of the tech world said: She thinks companies such as Facebook and Google should be *paying us* for all the time we spend online and all the billions and billions of bits of data we offer up—free, no charge—they can sell. Commerce, my friends. It's alive. It's thriving.

I'm grateful to topiary hair styles (a word borrowed from "the horticultural practice of training perennial plants by clipping the foliage"), especially on men. You know, the way they pile their hair on top of their heads, shaped just so.

After years and years of male politicians and male-dominated movies, I'm grateful for a handful of new stateswomen and female-centered series featuring badass women. I'm not talking about *Madame Secretary*, a calming series of domestic bliss, a la *Father Knows*

Best. I'm thinking of *Rita*, a Danish comedy-drama (warning: subtitles) about a headstrong, outspoken, unconventional teacher. If this show is any indication, the Danes are not afraid to confront dicey issues. Rita is badass No. 1.

A close second is Marie Yovanovitch, the steely former ambassador to Ukraine who stood tall and spoke truth to Congress about what she saw and heard.

Finally, I have to hand it to libraries across the country that have enlisted the services of drag queens—DRAG QUEENS!—to enter the staid and serious domain of books to entertain children. They (the children) love it. The Drag Queen Story Hour nonprofit has 35 chapters in the United States and five overseas. The children are engaged. They see something a little bit different. They like the flash.

Heck, a few months ago I heard about a couple of drag queens who showed up at a charity bingo event. In Statesboro. As in Georgia. Drag queens: They've become a mainstream thing. Who'd a thunk it? "There are more things in heaven and earth, Horatio, than are dreamt of in your philosophy." That's from Shakespeare, where more than once males assume the roles of females but are never called drag queens. "The more things change the more they stay the same." Some French guy said that.

12/22/19

2 / *Curating the day (Or do you say 'literally'?)*

The world gets curiouser and curiouser, said Alice (in Wonderland), a term firmly ensconced in our lexicon thanks to the English writer Lewis Carroll. And that was in 1865. What would Carroll think today? Here I am, out and about, harboring my occasional fantasy about playing tennis, searching for tennis balls, resisting a drive to DICK'S Sporting Goods.

"Oh, we discontinued them," said one clerk in a drug store in midtown in early October. "We're getting ready for Christmas. We needed the space."

"Tennis balls?" said someone else in another establishment. "You mean the kind you put under walkers? Yep. Aisle five."

"Yes, we have them." This from the third place I tried. "Right here," he said, walking me to the pet section, pointing to an actual fuzzy yellow tennis ball wrapped in plastic. "My dog loves them."

What planet are we on?

If shopping doesn't amuse you, there's always the joy of finding old words in new settings. Take the word "curator," as in so-and-so is scheduled to curate an art show. Only now this familiar verb has gone viral. Lately, I've seen it used to describe someone who is curating one's life, one's memories, one's regrets, as in this sentence, which I found in a book review, "She had started to curate her mind." Originally, I spotted it in a news story about 42 priests in Buffalo who were accused of sexual abuse. The original list had the names of 117 priests, but, as the bishop's administrative assistant explained, "The list was curated to deceive the public."

"To curate" is the new "to obfuscate."

On a lighter note, what about the term "smart casual"? In case you've been reading Proust and hadn't noticed the change in language or appropriate behavior, this is a thing. I was invited to a party this summer where the invitation offered this as the suggested dress. "Smart casual" is "polished yet relaxed." You're wearing garments that are elegant and comfortable as opposed to "business casual" (that's a thing, too), without the suit and tie.

Then there's the word "literally." This used to be reserved for people of a certain sophistication, a certain élan. Now it's coming from the mouths of seven-year-olds. Or younger. "I literally almost choked when I tasted almond butter," said one five-year-old I know, so accustomed was he to peanut butter.

Where is this coming from? I assumed from the parents of said five- and seven-year-olds.

Maybe. But when did they—and the rest of us—start using it as a fill-in for "figuratively"?

There is an explanation a thirtysomething named Sarah told me the other day. It comes from a TV series from 2009—*Parks and Recreation*—when Rob Lowe, playing Chris Traeger, used this word in an exaggerated form hundreds of times. There's even a T-shirt with the term. You can literally order and receive it in 24 hours.

Then there's the term for when you try to unsubscribe or get yourself off some email that just won't stop following you around. "You have been added to our suppression list," the response goes. I don't know about you but I've never had a good feeling about the word "suppression." I associate it with the wish to quell or crush, as in communist activities.

Same with the word "misuse." Is this really what Thunderbolt wanted when they posted this note on the men's room in the W.E. Honey Park: "Closed due to misuse"?

Occasionally I'll read the wedding announcements in the New York Times. Lots of second marriages, lots of people in professions I have never heard of. But many, it seems, are tying the knot in "self-uniting" ceremonies. Right under our noses, this too has become a thing: couples getting married without the presence of a third-party officiant. It's nondenominational, a method, so says Wikipedia, referred to as a Quaker marriage. Some states allow this, some don't.

I tried using a colloquial term like that with the police officer who stopped me a week ago when I failed to make a complete stop on Montgomery Street before turning right.

"I guess I did a rolling stop," I said, trying to break the ice.

"Or a California stop," he answered.

We were connecting. I was on a roll.

"Are you liking this police work?" I asked the oh-so-serious officer who looked to be 12.

"Yeah," he said.

"New on the force?"

"Yep."

"What? A week?" I pushed.

"A month," he said.

He gave me a warning.

I literally almost hugged him.

11/13/19

3 / Golf Carts, Man Buns, and Tennis Shoes (A rotary phone anyone?)

Forget Aquarius. This is the age of golf carts (on streets), man buns (on men), mullets (universal). Raise your hand if you like any of those three? Mine is not raised. How do these trends start?

Golf carts belong on the golf course. They don't even belong there. People should walk—except when golf courses intersect with houses, gated communities, neighborhoods with extended garages and bike paths. It must start when your neighbor gets a tricked-out golf cart (kind of like barbecue grills), and you think, "Hey, that looks like fun." Overnight, it's the invasion of the golf carts. Not lit. Not licensed. Party-mobiles.

Golf carts belong up there with tennis shoes.

"Nice shoes," I said to a stranger while waiting for the pedestrian light to change.

"Thanks," she said. "I love new tennis shoes."

"Oh," I said, always looking for people to play tennis with. "Where do you play?"

"Oh, I don't play tennis," she said. "Never have. I just call them that."

She might just as well have called them "gym shoes," another common term (back when there was gym class), and I could have related.

Golf carts, tennis shoes, rotary phones. All the same.

"If you have a rotary phone please stay on the line," says the automated message from the public library.

Rotary phones are right up there with encyclopedias, phone books and channels.

"What channel is it on?" we used to ask about a certain television program when there were four or five clear choices.

Soon we'll be adding man buns to that list.

"Mommy, what's a man bun?"

Man buns started with men who have thinning hair or receding hairlines—or maybe (not to be too cynical) with hairdressers looking to increase their clientele. The result is strangely architectural and interesting. I find myself staring at them, thinking of the time and money spent on getting the parallel lines just so. Only they don't see me staring. They see an older woman looking at them. We don't count. You gotta hand it to these metrosexuals: they want to have fun with their body, too. They already have their across-the-body man bags and their man caves; they might as well have an expensive man bun to match.

Mullets? Toss 'em to the fish.

In the whole scheme of messy things in the world none of the above much matters, does it? Just commerce as usual.

But the cost of chocolate: now there's something to complain about. A regular Kit Kat, the treat you would snag at 10 a.m. when you got gas (standing behind someone buying lottery tickets) after you had been up for hours, that little bit of chocolate that used to cost 50 cents? Now it's up to $1.75.

Who can eat candy after Halloween anyway? Not me. That's too bad because there's so much around, especially since my new favorite four-year-old—a Power Ranger, don't you know, in mind and costume—left over a bunch of stuff even though he carefully announced (with me translating) in his sweet little voice to everyone handing out candy: "Do they have peanuts? I'm allergic to peanuts."

Except for the drive-by parents in cars, hovering in the middle of the street at the end of the night while their teens got what they could, it was a great Halloween. Plenty of animal masks. Plenty of powerful folk heroes, a multitude of TV/comic book/video characters I've never heard of and no politicians, although I did read about a certain woman who was running for president who dressed up as…president.

Best of all, although no one gives out fruit ("yuk") or nickels ("Daddy, what's this?"), many of the costumed children who showed up at our Parkside house were heard to say, "Thank you." You can't beat that. If they didn't say, "Thank you," the aforementioned Power Ranger four-year-old, who is allergic to peanuts and trained and mannered, was heard to query, "What do you say?"

The morning after, squashed mini candy bars littered the sidewalk and the seventh game of the World Series ended the way it should have—in Houston's favor. I'd like to think it was José Altuve, the five-foot-six-inch second baseman from Venezuela ("although he's probably five-feet-five," one of the broadcasters—maybe Joe Buck—said) who brought it home.

I never heard such said about such a short ballplayer. But no man bun for José Altuve. No mullet, either.

11/12/17

4 / *Deplorable or Adorable (Excuse the Hillary reference; this time it's dogs)*

On the subject of human beings coming across stray animals in despair, I've always said there are two groups of folks: those who stop to help and those who don't. You know the scene: a dog trying to squeeze between cars on a road with everyone honking at once, a stray hovering around in the lane with no tags. I'm in the second category. I can always think of a good reason not to stop. It's not my best quality but somehow I can always find an excuse to look away, not to intervene, not to volunteer. Let someone else take care of it. I've got enough on my plate. Someone else will step up.

A few months ago, through some simple twist of fate (a Bob Dylan lyric, a Bob Dylan song) I agreed to foster two dogs, Gina and Sweetie, all this before setting eyes on them, before defining "foster." That was before Thanksgiving. I still have the dogs, but in truth I have no idea how this will end up. My heart sort of sank when I saw them. Gina, a puppy mill dog, the seven-year-old, is blind in one eye, bone-thin, needy, in possession of an amazing vertical jump and a chronic cough from a heart murmur. The first few days she didn't hesitate to show her teeth when someone got a little too close or leaned in a little too fast.

The other, Sweetie, is 12. She is bow-legged with short, tiny, shrimplike legs, a curved, skinny tail in the shape of a smile, a big belly and a pint-sized head that forgot to grow with the rest of her. My friend Jane calls her Chubs. Her big, soft, short-haired chest nearly scrapes the ground. She reminds me of a sea lion without the flippers. Both dogs have expressive stand-up ears, always at attention. One has never missed a meal, the other is so-so about food.

They are not especially attractive. There's something regrettable—deplorable?—about them. There's something sad about them. They've outlived their owners. One fell to Alzheimer's and a daughter whose apartment didn't allow dogs. The other had a hip replacement and could no longer do right by the dog.

There goes the house if we get them, I thought, selfishly. They're old. They smell. They bark. They whimper. Sometimes they can't hold it.

There goes my time. In my grief over losing two dogs in one year, I still remember the subsequent pleasure at not having to get home to walk them, not having to enlist neighbors to fill in when I was away, not sweeping up dog hair, not apologizing for how the house smells.

Isn't this great? I'd say to no one in particular. *Not being tied down. A peaceful house that stays clean.*

After we got comfortable together, I started walking them in the lane without a leash. I watched Gina break away from my side and do the 100-yard dash long enough to forget her fear of being left alone. She was a child with a child's excitement and bounce. She stopped when I called her. I watched Sweetie's little legs carry her rounded rump as she explored every plant, so curious was she, so active.

They were growing on me.

But I still wasn't certain. Then I took an afternoon nap and that was it. In seconds, Gina had jumped up and was lying on my belly. She circled around for a while, then settled in, her breathing matching my own. Her weight (slight as it is) felt comfortable, grounding. In minutes she was emitting a pleasant, satisfied snore. The winter sun filtered through the window. A paw, so light, so slight, rested on my hand as if to say, "We are in this together, right? We're a team." I felt content.

Later, after hoisting Sweetie onto the couch, she who lacks the necessary vertical jump, I stare into her graying face, her white muzzle, her soulful dark eyes and ask, "Who are you? What were you like in the prime of your life? When did you get this big belly? Are you happy? Are you remembering your earlier owner?"

For now, we agree, we will carry on. We will debate the meaning of "fostering" at another time. We will—in Baba Ram Dass' blessed memory—be here now.

12/29/19

5 / *Frida Burrita*
Taco Chalupa
(The dog, the myth, the legend)

This is how it went.

I fed her. I walked her three times a day. I gave her fresh water. I talked to her. I set up playdates. I offered encouragement when she was down. I washed her bedding, fluffed her pillow, helped fill out her college application and drove her to salsa lessons (not really). But by 3 p.m., maybe an hour early (she didn't want to be late), she would perch on the back of the couch in full view of the street and start her vigil.

It was time for Carmela, her other mother—her true love—to return home from work. When she could no longer jump on the couch anymore or when we moved the couch, she would flatten out, belly to the floor, head aimed toward the street waiting for the front door to open. After that, I was chopped liver, nothing more, unless she wanted something (more food, more water, another outing); then she would follow me from room to room, trying to catch my eye, trying to send out the message, the reminder.

It was pathetic. She was her mama's girl, always and forever, ever since Jenna, her favorite mama's daughter, stepped in and saved her from a disgruntled and clueless owner who had just been told she was a Chihuahua, not a Huskie, that she would be a lover, not an attack dog, a dog who would weigh 12 pounds, not 150 pounds. Ever since she came home to Mama No. 1.

I was forever more an afterthought.

She was Frida Burrita Taco Chalupa. To Rob-Rob, our neighbor across the street, she was Frida Chalupa.

In 16 years, she never bit anyone, delivered kisses to anyone who asked, made love her mantra. She was well-mannered, well-behaved and considerate to the end. When her lumps of cancer kept spreading along her belly, interfering with her highly developed skills of communication, and she could no longer "hold it," she was very good about using the puppy pads we put out for her. Her countenance remained strong, her tail high.

"We'll know when it's time," we said to one another. "We'll know when she no longer wants to live." And, speaking euphemistically, "We will do something about it. We will help her along."

The day came closer. She became more compliant, more snuggly, more like the undercover dog she had been at the beginning when she could still jump on the bed, when she would scoot under the covers. (How she breathed, I'll never know). The tail that always nodded and swayed started to droop. Her eyes clouded over. Her gaze took on a distant aspect, fixing, as it would, on a point way far away.

It didn't matter. Denial is strong. I watched where I stepped (especially in the middle of the night or in the morning), ready to pick up any droppings. I didn't complain. We positioned puppy pads at strategic spots, experimented with different brands of stain and odor removers, used different detergents. We swept, mopped, sponged and wiped.

When the time arrived, we knew it. She wasn't eating much, drinking even less. Her spirit seemed to be leaving her body. We'll take her in the next morning, we agreed. That night around 3 a.m. Mama No. 1 thought she heard something. She got up, cradled Frida in her lap, told her she loved her and went back to bed.

The next morning, I got up early. Frida was sprawled on her side behind my bicycle wheel, legs out in normal fashion, mouth slightly open. Something was not right. I bent down and looked closer. Ever considerate, ever thoughtful, she did what no animal, no pet I've ever known has done: she had died in her sleep.

3/16/19

6 / *Dispatching chickens*
(Chicken fricassee?
I don't think so)

I've never been emotionally attached to my chickens. I know that's not particularly p.c., but there you have it. I don't name them. I don't pretend to commune with them. I've never had a special pet chicken who moved into the house, drank out of the dog bowl, slept in the bed. I just like to have them around. I like the way they kick up the dirt. I like their up and down pecking. They're industrious, good role models, good company. I like their gentle clucking and then the amazing whoo-hoo-look-what-I've-done sounds when they lay an egg (and why not: what a feat; every 23 hours no less).

The silence I experienced the other day when I walked through the garden with a cup of feed and a day's worth of vegetable scraps—banana peels, celery tips, pepper innards—was all the more ominous. Not good, I said to myself, because if they're not particularly bright, chickens do know the sound (and maybe the smell?) I make when I arrive in the morning and walk through the garden; they do know those sounds mean FOOD.

This morning there was no clucking. The silence was heavy, like after a sharply drawn breath.

It's funny how we can't take in tragedy all at once. We see bits and pieces, like the time I got into my car to head for Key West for a week. The side mirror had been broken, shards of glass were everywhere, my glove box had been opened and emptied. Yet all I saw when I opened the door was the lighter (remember those? I don't think cars have them anymore). It was lying on the black floor mat. That's strange, I said to myself. I don't remember that sitting there before.

Then I saw the car instruction manual on the floor, then the open glove box, then some cassettes. Finally I saw the shattered side mirror and I put two and two together and I cried. Someone had broken into my car. I was offended. I was violated.

The first chicken I saw was sprawled in the dusty floor of the coop. Nothing unusual there—at first blush. They like to take dirt baths. Then I saw the big red hole in her back. She wasn't moving. The second chicken was quivering. The third was hiding under the coop, trembling. All had been under some kind of attack.

Now, I don't have any trouble burying a dead animal. I've done that lots of times, sometimes with tears, sometimes not. But animals with one foot in the grave? Time to dial a friend. I called Jake. I'll be right over, he said. He arrived, on his bike, with a plastic bag, ready to take them home where he would "dispatch" them.

What a civilized word: dispatch.

I hung around, a little dazed, a little stunned. The silence of the coop was deafening. But what happened? Who got in and how? It didn't take long before I saw the culprits, the miscreants. The last time I lost chickens it was to a husky that got out of a backyard. This time it was a pair of marauding rat terriers. No collars. They had returned to the scene of the crime, sniffing around, looking for a little more. I stayed to see how they got in and out, and I made a note to fix it.

I'm going to get chickens again, just not this month. That I know. I also know I wasn't quite ready to go to lunch when Jake invited me.

"I think I'll take a pass," I said.

It was a little too soon, a little too personal.

4/29/12

7 / *Toxicity,*
thy name is Hillary
(I'm with her)

There are many ways in which we human beings can argue, to make ourselves right. Is it the War Between the States or the Civil War? The Stones vs. the Beatles? Coke or Pepsi? The Wolverines or the Buckeyes?

Less important (to me, at least) is one's preferred architectural form. "Which shape do you like the best?" Benny, my favorite 6-year-old, asks from the confines of a stall in a public bathroom as I wait nearby.

"My favorite shake?" I say.

"No! Shape!"

"Shake?" I try again. "Like, strawberry shake?"

"Shape!" He repeats, followed by, "Oh, never mind."

"Shape," an exasperated woman from another stall yells.

"Triangle," I say quickly, trying to regain some semblance of credibility. "What's yours?"

"Cube," he returns quietly, as if to say all is forgiven between us.

None of those differences of opinion compares to what happens when you mention the word "Hillary," as in Clinton, as in First Lady, as in Chelsea. Heaven forbid you should say anything positive about her. Some of my best friends—intelligent, caring, cogent, free-thinking people—hate her. P.S., these are people who usually vote Democratic to boot.

If I dared move into contentious territory with the expected fireworks, I would urge these best friends of mine to watch the new documentary "Hillary." And then I would ask: What is so polarizing about a woman who speaks her mind, who does her research, who is articulate, smart, hard-working, committed?

In one review I read about this four-part series, now available on Hulu, Newt Gingrich, the former Speaker of the House, that moral, upright, principled politician, refused to be interviewed and said, "I would rather stick a needle in my eye than talk to you about Hillary Clinton in a documentary."

Is it because she kept her married name Rodham when she married Bill Clinton? Because she kept on working as a lawyer when she moved to Little Rock after their marriage (a move her best friends from Wellesley College and Yale Law School thought she was crazy to do because she was so smart and had such a huge future in front of her)?

Is it because she articulated the country's problem with delivering health care and dared to come up with a plan—a start, a beginning, something?

That she dared to address the elephant in the room? Should she have done the work and handed it over to a man, who then could have pretended he did the work? That would have been the "smart" thing if she wanted to advance the cause. Women have followed that course for eons.

Let's remember a few things. Remember the scene in *Hidden Figures* when one of the three women scientists had to run outside in the rain to find a bathroom for "colored" people? This was in the 1960s.

Is it so hard to realize women—and people of color—have always been held to a higher standard than men? Women must not raise their voices. They must not come off as the smartest in the room. They must be empathetic but not emotional. They have to endure hours and hours of makeup sessions, hair sessions, focus groups of what to wear on stage.

Their male counterparts? They comb their hair—maybe. They brush their teeth—maybe. They slip into a jacket and take the stage. No one is telling them to smile more. No one is applying lipstick just so. Women get pilloried if they're too cold or too sentimental.

Yes, she said, "I could have stayed home and made cookies but what I decided to do was fulfill my profession." This was a bad thing to say—very, very bad.

Is there any wonder after that brouhaha she decided to slip on a mask, to be cautious with her words?

Her name—Hillary—is almost as polarizing as another word, feminism, and maybe that's why the film is so good, so relevant. That and the recent crash and burn of another female politician, Elizabeth Warren, make this a very compelling and frustrating movie to watch. Those same people who say they don't like being lectured to—a common complaint directed toward Warren—have no complaint with Bernie Sanders' relentless hectoring. Warren is saying the same thing, but her message gets drowned out. If a woman shouts, she is hysterical. A man? He's passionate.

For some of us who lived through the last half of the 20th century, the documentary is history. It's a reminder. And it's painful. I just kept thinking, what a shame, what a waste. Not necessarily about Clinton or Warren, but about all the smart women out there who could move this world just a little bit further. Would that be so bad?

3/14/20

8 / *Babies:*
they offer hope
(I think)

Is it just me or does it seem as if there is an inordinate number of babies around these days, slung on a daddy's back, snug against a mama's chest, tucked in a walker? They're everywhere. At the Saturday Forsyth Farmers' Market, in Daffin Park, on the streets. More fathers with babies too. (Fathers without jobs? Perhaps).

With all the uncertainty in the world, people—smart people—still have enough faith in the future to introduce another soul into the mix. Imagine putting down on a form "2017" as the year you were born. And they're having more than one child, too. Two, three. They just keep popping them out.

The most popular names for girls this year? Emma, Ava, Olivia, Sophia. Must be something about words ending in an "a". Just to prove a point, the next three are Isabella, Mia and Amelia. Three more "a"s on the end. Boys? Liam, Noah, Logan, Lucas. Three out of four starting with an "L," followed by Mason, Ethan, Oliver.

No one-syllable names. No Bob, John, Ted or Jim. No Jane either, until you get down to number 288. Boo-hoo. No Nancy, Suzy, Marcy or Judy—the names of my four high school friends from the Sixties. Paisley, however, is ranked number 43, after Skylar, Aurora and Savannah, before Lillian, Brooklyn (not to be confused with Brooklynn, which comes in at 170) and Hazel. For the record, I don't know anyone with those names (well, maybe Savannah but she changed it).

No Rose either (that was my mother's name) or any of the names of my aunts: Betty, Dorothy, Mildred, Trudy. No Celia or Eva (my grandmothers' names). No Beverly (my mother's best friend) or Dolly, Jeanette or Loris (her bridge partners).

Certainly, on the boys' side, no Mannie (that was my father's name) or Herman, Mickey or Ben (his brothers) or Harry, Saul or Lou (my mother's brothers). No Lou-from-Windsor, either. He was another uncle, not to be confused with Lou-from-Detroit. Even those names speak to another generation.

I could worry about these babies. How will they learn to tie their shoes with Velcro around? What about telling time non-electronically, with just a second hand and a minute hand? Will they still do cartwheels? Will the almighty dollar hold the same allure?

I'm not going to worry. I look at them and I'm hopeful. I'm betting they'll be against conspicuous consumption. We already know the happiest people are those making up to $75,000 a year. Any more than that introduces stress and the need for more.

I'm thinking these babies, when all grown up, will live in smaller houses, drive smaller cars and live in smaller towns. They may share houses. Money will not be such an issue. They'll call storage units stupid and wasteful. They'll wonder why we don't have more and wider bike paths, more buses. They'll look at the bottleneck in Pooler and say, "What was the matter with you?"

They'll think it's ridiculous we don't teach music and art in school. Every day. "What were you thinking?" They'll wonder why there are so few statues of women, why out of 5,193 historic figures on street corners and parks in the United States only 394 are women.

I hate to be around when they see how we bungled health care. By the time they're adults, it will be "Medicare for all." It's the only logical way to go. People not on Medicare don't understand how easily it works. All the other options will seem wasteful, discriminatory and thick-headed. Get ready. They'll be saying, "You mean you let the pharmaceutical companies and the insurance honchos run the show? Shame on you, Mom. Bad, Dad."

They'll look at our prison systems and say, "Don't you see it's just a money-maker for those in small towns? Or racism, the dominant class versus the subordinates? It's so obvious. That all those petty

miscreants you incarcerated with a joint or two will come out prac-
ticed, hardcore criminals? Is that what you meant to do? You mean
you didn't teach them anything when you had them there, a captured
audience? They just watched television all day and worked out? Then
when they got out, they could never vote again? Ludicrous."

They're not mine, these babies, but seeing them gives me hope.
And this from someone who wavers somewhere between joy and despair. Maybe it's the blue sky today or the cooler temperatures or the
thought of Thanksgiving, but somehow I'm feeling a light at the end
of the Trumpian tunnel. You watch. These babies will have our backs.
They'll be eating more garbanzo beans than meat. They'll be turning
front yards into vegetable gardens and side yards into orchards. They'll
be growing more lemons, more oranges, more Fuyu persimmons than
they know what to do with. They'll be sporting bumper stickers that
say, "I'm already against the next war." They'll be sharing.

11/19/17

9 / Gardening: It's not a competition (But why are her okra plants so tall?!)

A single surviving (but still firm and tasty) Vidalia onion I forgot to pull months ago; a stand of obedience plants that expanded from one offering during April's plant swap, something I jammed into the garden before an innocent plant swapper might think it was up for grabs; a surprise gathering of reseeding arugula I smelled seconds before I saw it; a few precious and promising sorrel plants; a hardy group of basil plants. That's about all I have to report from my summer garden.

That's a pretty pathetic assessment for someone who wrote a book on gardening. Maybe the title—*I Grew It My Way, How Not To Garden*—says it all. But I still stand by it. Gardening is not a competition. It's an activity. It's something you do for yourself. It's an art form. It never ends and it's never perfect. How many times have you complimented someone on their garden, only to hear, "Yes, but you should have seen it yesterday?"

To garden is to be outside, to wear old clothing, to get your hands into dirt, to move into downward dog and cat-and-cow, away from the yoga studio and off the yoga mat. It's to haul water from the rain barrel in five-gallon buckets instead of going to the gym and lifting weights. It's to ponder, to experiment, to smell hidden ginger blooms, to mess with worms (let's hear it for vermicomposting!). It's to see a butterfly circling around the salvia, to sit on the front porch early in the morning and watch a mama mockingbird—and a papa too—tend to their fledglings. It's to hear a woodpecker hunting for bugs, to feel the approaching rain, to stop and admire the acrobatic squirrels. It's to be in the moment.

OK, so the statuesque, robust frangipani has still not bloomed. Ever. The mint struggles and is on the road to disappearing. Everyone else's okra is double the size of mine. The night-blooming cereus, while looking healthy, is barren. The Padrón peppers—oh, I wanted those Padróns—disappointed. The lime trees, so very tall, so very promising for gin and tonics, have produced nothing. And the invading muscadine vine, a newcomer that is starting to overpower the passion vine (which is saying something) has moved into first place in territory-grabbing. But hey, where are the muscadines? Not fair, as a seven-year-old I know might say, folding her arms and stomping her feet.

Still, the sprawling American beautyberry astounds (and keeps the mosquitoes away). The handsome sunflowers returned, early and happy, with no coaxing at all. Same with the sugarcane. The beauty of the low-to-the-ground pinecone ginger—or do you say shampoo ginger?—stops dog walkers in their tracks. The scarlet hibiscus, with those pointed marijuana-looking leaves, gets some attention and demands some answers. The trail of Cherokee beans—planted in April—may still produce some product. I'm starting to spot some red "modified leaves" on the ground under the banana trees, only to look up and see the start of a hand of bananas. Will they have time to grow? We don't know. And does it matter? And while the edible starchy tubers of the voodoo lily plant may make it into the kitchen in a pinch (a serious pinch) I think I'll just sit back and enjoy it—wherever it came from (probably the plant swap)—as a curiosity.

But now it's time to think of winter. It's time to pull errant weeds, scrape around the bottom of the compost pile for some good, black, rich soil, move it over to growing areas and start preparing the ground for another group of vegetables—onions, garlic, collards, kale, carrots, rutabagas and maybe cabbage. It's time to start all over again.

11/19/17

10 / *Just push the button,*
says Golda Meir
(But don't expect me
to change a tire)

How about this flu? Is it over yet? It's kind of freaking me out. All those viruses; I'm starting to think the Russians are behind it. Do we need a committee to investigate this?

How about that Roger Federer at the Australian Open? Thirty-six years old and still standing, still winning, still weeping after he's done winning. And no whining when he's not winning. Tennis continues to be the closest thing we have to a gladiator sport, two armed (with rackets) combatants in the ring. Mano a mano, hand to hand. Since none of my cable channels run the big tournaments, I have to go up to the tennis courts at Forsyth Park to get my fix. Ringside seats, free admittance. There are some lean and mean and young players there. And no commercials.

How about these women? I did not make it to this year's march in Washington, D.C. (it was a perfect day to plant sugar snaps, one of those must-get-my-hands-in-the-dirt days) but who could miss the post-march signs, the art, the fervor, the energy? One million people marched. "Resistance is not futile," one sign read. Another said, "A woman's place is in your face." Something is going on here. It's not the first time we've heard from women, but in this latest version I'd say the movement has legs. If we don't have a female president, we do have lots of women running for office, speaking their minds, being heard. If we don't have a truth and reconciliation commission, as they have in South Africa, we are starting to have our own form of truth and reconciliation.

It's about time. Did I think twice in the mid-'60s when my high school principal told me not to wear pants when I showed up for my first job as a high school English teacher? No. I did as I was told (for a year).

Did we think it odd that women were kept from broadcasting positions because their voices were deemed too thin or their intellect lacked depth? No. Most of the time these broadcasters—men, women alike—are just reading the news anyway. Trust me, it was a big deal back then when women sat behind the reporting desk, when women did the reporting.

Would I refuse a man's offer to change my tire? Heck no. But I do know how to use jumper cables to start my car. Red is positive, black is negative. And I do have a good mechanic.

And we do have a great, new word at our disposal: mansplaining. Would that we had this word, this awareness years ago to deal with all the one-sided "conversations" we've had with men, waiting for them to get to the point. But no. We just stood there mute or hushed or talked over while they offered those loud and long explanations disguised in that "I know best" attitude. We just stood there and endured the hectoring, the swagger, the bluster, the interruptions, all the while thinking, "Boring! When can I get out of here?"

The other night at a concert, a man behind us was speaking LOUDLY and OFTEN with no awareness of how his voice was carrying. "Mansplaining," I whispered to a friend next to me. Would that I could have told him.

The good news is women seem to be waking up from a long, long slumber. So far, 325 nonincumbent women are running for the U.S. House compared to 167 two years ago, with 38 running for positions in the Senate compared to 16 in 2016. This is just the beginning.

There's plenty of room for women to rise in the ranks of leadership. But it's good to remember none of it is new. Women have been making their voices heard for a long time.

Witness Golda Meir, Israel's first female prime minister, who had to endure plenty of mansplaining, I'm sure. She was born in Ukraine and, an early immigrant, grew up in Milwaukee. As a Jew, as a lifelong battler for the state of Israel, she liked to call herself an atheist who identified culturally with Judaism. There's a bold description.

The other day I came across the following passage in a biography I'm reading about her (*Lioness: Golda Meir and the Nation of Israel*, by Francine Klagsbrun).

When asked how she rose so far in the ranks of leadership, she answered, "I don't know anything about leadership. I can only tell you that I was going to the theater one evening and I got on the elevator. Nobody in the elevator bothered to move. So, I pressed the button. That's all I can say about leadership."

Last I checked, there are still plenty of buttons that need pressing.

2/7/18

As we ramp up for another war, it's hard not to think of Muhammad Ali, who refused to go to Vietnam (*"No Viet Cong never called me nigger"*), a felony that the U.S. Supreme Court eventually overturned. A few months ago, Carmela and I went to The Studio Museum in Harlem, where we saw this Glenn Ligon black-and-white neon piece based on a poem of Ali's. As the story goes, Ali, who now has Parkinson's, was addressing the senior class at Harvard when someone yelled out, "Give us a poem." So the boxer known for his bon mots ("Float like a butterfly, sting like a bee") did, producing on the spot what is known as the shortest poem in the English language: "Me, We," expressing, I suppose, that the fate of the individual is linked in a broad way to the community at large.

Ali was an unusual man.

MAY 4, 2013

PEOPLE

1 / *Anne and Sigmund Hudson*

A few weeks ago, with nearly sixty boxes packed, stacked, wrapped, numbered and annotated in a notebook the way only a mathematician would, Sigmund Hudson, 82, stopped his moving chores long enough to ride his bicycle to Home Depot. He needed a light bulb.

"He's careful," said Anne, his wife of 59 years. She did not seem concerned. Anne, 87, had just returned from a Saturday women's gathering at St. Matthew's Episcopal Church on Martin Luther King, Jr. Boulevard, where she's been a member for decades. Safety on the road is one thing. Taking the time and having the presence of mind to pedal a bike—instead of burning some gas to save a little time—is something else.

But that's how Sigmund and Anne roll, quietly, consistently, without making too much noise about what they're doing. They are not preachy. They are not moralizing. They do what they think is right for themselves and for the environment.

The Hudsons, longtime civic activists, have left their mark. In 1976, four years after moving to Savannah, when they and several others saw that Baldwin Park needed a little tidying up, they formed a neighborhood association. Today, that kind of community relationship seems obvious. But not then.

Decades later, the Baldwin Park Neighborhood Association is still going strong, but it will be without the Hudsons. Last week, Anne and Sigmund headed for St. Louis to live with their son and daughter-in-law.

They are leaving behind a playbook on how to live. For decades, they've made it a point to welcome new people to the neighborhood, visit neighbors who were sick, bring food to those who were old, host wine and hors d'oeuvres gatherings for people at the Armstrong Campus of Georgia State University—in their home. They've housed musicians who had come to town to join the symphony but hadn't secured living arrangements, tended the garden at the Flannery O'Connor Childhood Home, and donated bicycles, tents, blankets and sleeping bags to the Community of St. Joseph, a ministry for the homeless.

They volunteered at the Bull Street public library, where they formed a book club that met regularly. Every Monday, Sigmund rode his bike to Union Mission, a downtown Savannah organization to address homelessness, to do any repairs that needed tending.

Anne knitted cloth clowns for newborns in the neighborhood and offered math tutorials to children who were not catching on. For my annual Chanukah party, she sewed tablecloths, napkins and potholders made out of menorah-decorated fabric.

A month ago, at the Flannery O'Connor birthday celebration and parade, a grinning Sigmund carried a hand-painted sign with a Flannery quote that read, "Accepting oneself does not preclude an attempt to become better."

The Hudsons have lived their lives consciously, with humor, with intention. When Anne taught mathematics at the former Armstrong State University, she didn't drive. She walked up a few blocks and caught the Abercorn Street bus. "A good time to grade papers," she said, as if to imply *no big deal*. "You really got to know the bus drivers, too."

It pays to make such personal connections. Once, by mistake, Anne left a briefcase of papers at the bus stop. No problem. The driver knew who it belonged to. On his break, he popped into the Armstrong cafeteria and returned it to her.

When Sigmund, also a professor of mathematics, taught at Savannah State University, he rode his bicycle to campus. Later, after getting another degree, he taught computer science at Armstrong.

While Anne was the first woman to earn a doctorate in mathematics from Tulane University (where Sigmund also got his doctorate), she and her husband would be the last people who would ever want to be called "doctor." Similarly, while the rest of us might say "math" (one syllable), neither would ever say the word without pronouncing all four distinct syllables. Math-e-ma-tics.

The Hudsons are no strangers to modest living. For decades, they have summered in the wild on their hilly, rural property in New Hampshire, far before any internet or decent phone connectivity. They slept in a raised tent on a wooden platform and cooked over a fire. During the day, they might walk up a few yards to a small free-standing room that Sigmund built. There they would sit in comfortable chairs and read. One year, Anne picked and identified plants and flowers as a community art project. In 2005, they finally gave in and moved into a modest cabin with indoor plumbing and electricity.

Recently, they had been giving some thought to downsizing. A few years ago, when notified they had won a Panhandle Slim poster at a Flannery O'Connor fundraising event, they turned it down. "We're not buying anymore art," Sigmund said. "Give it to someone else."

A few days ago, I found a present from Sigmund on my porch: a copy of Steve Bender and Felder Rushing's seminal book *Passalong Plants*, with the inscription to "pass it along." Since I already have a copy, I will pass his along.

For years they were known as a two-person litter patrol for the regular pickup walks around their neighborhood. It was what they did. Nothing sexy. Nothing grand. No T-shirts. No Facebook or social media recognition. Just an everyday act by a couple of modest and gentle people paying attention to their footprint in the world.

4/6/19

2 / *Homeless in Savannah: Meet Don*

If it weren't for the bags (and the teeth: he doesn't have any), Don could be any one of us. His sun-bleached hair is parted and nicely combed. His glasses, though sometimes crooked, hide warm blue eyes. His black shoes and socks match; his pants and shirt look worn but clean. They're nice bags, one a stylishly designed black backpack with padded shoulder straps, the other a sturdy new blue satchel with two exterior zip pockets. But they're bags. And that, says Don, is what sets him apart.

"People see the bags and they don't talk to me," he said the other day with no particular rancor as we sipped iced tea in front of the Foxy Loxy Café on Bull Street. His face was calm. "They look away."

The bags sat at his feet. They contain everything he owns: a couple shirts, some pants, a sweater, his phone charger, his books, his deodorant and shampoo, a baseball hat, his pillow, a blanket. He does not have a storage locker for memorabilia. He does not stash winter clothes in a friend's attic. He does not cram photo albums in his car. He doesn't have a car. He doesn't have a home.

Don sleeps on a bench downtown, a bench he was forced to leave during Hurricane Matthew's mandatory evacuation.

"Sometime around midnight a cop came by and said, 'It's either Carl Griffin Drive or Augusta,'" Don told me. "I was at Carl Griffin once—that's the Chatham County Sheriff's Office—and it's no fun. I was sleeping in a vacant house, and they didn't let me take my shoes when they handcuffed me. I had to walk back to town in some flimsy shoes they gave me and that didn't feel good."

Nowadays, most of the time the police don't bother him, he said, "unless it's a new one, a rookie, then they'll wake me up in the middle of the night and ask for my ID. I figure that's my civic responsibility, to be there for their training."

For the Hurricane Matthew evacuation, Don chose the bus to Augusta. He and about 20 others ended up at some middle school near Augusta Technical College. "I'm a pretty good meteorologist and I didn't think we had to leave. I guessed the last one right. I was living on Wilmington Island and went to my office in Thunderbolt. I had a small printing company. Sure enough, it passed over."

Don has not always slept on a public bench. When the printing company went bust, he moved to Jacksonville and worked for AOL, talking to customers, trying to convince them not to cancel their service. He worked for a pawn shop for a few years, operated a forklift, drove a cab, sold cell phones. He tried day labor, which might pay $50 a day. The last job he had was lifting concrete blocks. He didn't last long. "In one hour my arms were rubber," he said. He'd live in cheap hotels. When things got bad he'd go to Union Mission or places that took in homeless people.

"But I didn't like how I was treated," he said. "One night I remember I just started crying at how they talked to us and that was it for me."

Now his day is pretty regulated. His phone alarm wakes him up, he gathers his things and heads for Emmaus House, a program run by United Ministries of Savannah that feeds a hot meal to nearly 200 people four days a week and a bag lunch on Friday. He can take a shower there, too. Then he might catch the city shuttle or walk to the public library on Bull Street. Don's a reader. He figures he reads four books in five days. He'll check the free library in front of Brighter Day Natural Foods Market twice a day for books. He's fond of Tom Clancy, John Grisham, David Ellis ("You ever heard of him? He helped prosecute Rod Blagojevich in Chicago. He's gotten better.").

Don knows something about Chicago politics. He was a delegate to the state Democratic convention. And he coordinated the Democratic party in Illinois' Coles County, home to Eastern Illinois

University, where he finished three years of college.

"I'd go crazy if I couldn't read. I learned it from being a parent when I had to tune out everything, the TV, the internet. Now it's the bluster that's around me, all the jabbering. I've become a real loner."

At the library he reads his books, communicates with friends and his daughter via email, and he works on an internet game he hopes to market.

He reads two newspapers a day, the Savannah Morning News and USA Today, either at the library or in a hotel lobby. He knows to stash his bags and straighten up before he goes into the hotel. That way he can sit and read and use the bathroom. But that's the only time he leaves his bags out of his sight. When the library closes, he might go to City Market where he leans against a building and reads into the night, "across from the statue of Johnny Mercer who's reading a paper." He's friends with some restaurant employees who sometimes bring him food.

He rarely has more than a few bucks in his pocket. But he never begs. "I would never do that, never," he said. Every month he gets $194 in food stamps. Sometimes he sells (illegally) his stamps. Then he can buy cigarettes and sell those for some cash.

In two years he'll get Social Security, around $1,000 a month. But even then he's not inclined to go into a rooming house.

"It's a crappy way to retire, but you deal with the cards you've been dealt. It's not a normal life, but somehow or another you find a niche."

10/30/16

3 / Betty
and Sylvia

What do you do when you quit working? Who do you visit when your mother dies and your grandchildren live a zillion miles away in Montana? How do you expand your circle?

How do you learn Yiddish when you're a Baptist?

"Easy," said Betty Hodges. "You find someone like Sylvia."

"It was my lucky day when I met you," said Sylvia Dane-Kellogg.

It was *bashert*, Yiddish for "meant to be", or "destiny", when these two women—separated by decades, religions, experience—met.

"We were tying knots," said Sylvia, in her Brooklyn accent. "Making blankets."

"At Congregations in Service," said Betty finishing the sentence—in her broad Midwestern accent, where the "a" is prominent—which is what they do for one another. They finish thoughts, they share stories.

"Norman (Hirsch) was very involved with that, too," said Sylvia, "such a mensch."

"That's a good person, right?" asked Betty.

"Right," said Sylvia. "That was Norman. It's incredible one man could do what he did. He was a very good kisser, too, very affectionate."

Two days after Hirsch's funeral at Congregation Mickve Israel—and four days after Hirsch's unexpected death—Betty showed up at Sylvia's for their weekly Wednesday get-together. This week they were still talking about Norman, a friend to both of them.

"He was involved in things that mattered," said Sylvia. "He didn't push himself to the front. He did the work. I could see that from the day I met him and Julie (his wife)."

Sylvia was a few years younger then.

"Thereafter, I became aged and couldn't go to the activities," said Sylvia, who just turned 99.

"That's where we met," said Betty, 73. "When the group was making blankets. That's when you asked me to come visit."

And so she did.

"Betty keeps me informed about the world," said Sylvia. "But sometimes I think, 'Better I shouldn't know.'"

"It's been two—maybe three—birthdays that I've crossed paths with this beautiful lady," said Betty. "I couldn't do this kind of visiting with my mother. She lived out of state. This is perfect. I love her."

Betty worked for the City of Savannah for 23 years as a community development director. After short stints with the City of Tybee and a contractor, she found herself without a job, with too much time.

"That's when I decided, 'I have to do something.'"

Around that time Betty participated in a silent retreat at her church, First Baptist, "when we were given a charge to think how we can give back," she remembered. "I was the mission chair. When my pastor heard about Communities in Service—the group Norman helped form—he came to me and asked, 'Is this something we should do?' I didn't know much about it then, but I answered, 'I'm not interested if it's not interfaith.' Turns out it is: Muslim, Bahá'í, Jewish, Catholic, Unitarian, Unity.'"

But that wasn't enough.

Six years ago when Betty heard about LOVEMentors, a group formed by five churches on Skidaway Island, she got involved with that, too. LOVE stands for local, outreach, volunteer, educators. She and 120 other volunteers work in partnership with the Savannah-Chatham County Public School System to tutor below-grade-level elementary school students. Twice a week, Betty goes into the same school and meets with the same child.

"I'm borrowing grandkids," she said. "I'm not a trained educator. I'm a mother and a grandmother."

"We have another connection, too," said Betty. "Mickve Israel and First Baptist share a caterer, Bryan (Graves)."

"Allow me to interrupt," said Sylvia, interrupting. "And to disagree. I am fed by my visitors, like you."

"Another thing," Betty said, continuing the associations between the two of them. "One of my very best friends was Rabbi (Saul) Rubin's secretary. I took his 12-week class in Judaism. I wasn't ready for it to end."

That reminded Sylvia of the day Rabbi Robert Haas, from Mickve Israel, called and asked if he could visit.

"I thought, 'What does one speak to a rabbi about?' I was petrified. At the time, he wasn't married. I said, 'I'll find a bride for you.' He stayed three hours," she said.

Right about then Betty's phone "chirped."

"Your birds have sung," Sylvia said, in her deadpan manner.

"Time for handbell practice, dinner and church," said Betty.

"*Zei gezunt*," said Sylvia, as her Wednesday visitor prepared to go. Go in good health.

"*Zei gezunt*," said Betty, as if she'd been using that expression forever. "See you next week."

10/22/17

4 / *Robert and Millie:*
Movie night
on 41st Street

What do you get when you put a "gay guy and a sweet old lady" together? Movie night on East 41st Street. Of course.

At least that's how Robert Bush, the gay guy half of the couple, thinks some people might characterize the pair, tongue partially in cheek.

Robert, who just turned double-nickels (or 55), and Millie Dimmock, the sweet old lady half, two days short of 100, have been watching movies together for years, usually on Friday night. They call it date night. Dinner precedes the movie. A few nights ago, dinner was takeout Chinese, plenty of eggplant, egg foo young and Mongolian chicken with broccoli. No one ate before each said what the pair call "the gratefuls." This is something they both have been doing for years. Not surprisingly, most of the "gratefuls" center around good friends, good neighbors, good health.

Their gratitude goes back to 1996 when Robert, an attorney at Georgia Legal Services, bought a house—"my first house"—next door to Millie's. Millie and her late husband Joe moved to their Baldwin Park house in 1993.

They met soon after Robert moved in.

"It was 2 a.m. Right, Millie?" Robert started. "I came home late and couldn't find my key."

"Right," she said, confirming the memory as two old friends will do for one another. "You borrowed my ladder to climb up to the second-floor window. I stood out front and acted as your lookout in case the police came and thought you were trying to break in."

"It was raining, too," Robert said.

Dinner conversation started with quantum theory forensic physics.

"I think string theory makes more sense," Millie said.

"She's one of the most interesting people I know," Robert said. "If she's reading and doesn't know what something means, she turns to another book and looks it up."

No Google searching for Millie, the woman who sends out dozens of handwritten birthday cards every month.

"Books just make more sense," she said.

Somehow *The Iliad* came into the conversation.

"Millie's read it," Robert said.

"I've only read it in English," she said, feigning modesty. "I'm starting to forget some of the Greek I knew. And there were chapters I skipped."

These days she's reading *The Muslim Next Door*, which she calls "a real eye opener. But the Arabic language is so flowery it's hard to translate."

She's a little more familiar with Russian, which she studied for three years, mainly to facilitate her interest in painting Russian icons.

"Theology is so much easier in Russian," she said. "In that language one word says it. I went to a conference once about religion. All they talked about was what separated us. I was so disappointed at that."

As we talked Robert left the table and returned with a piece of Millie's art, painted in brilliant red.

"Who is it again?" Robert asked.

"St. George!" she said. "Can't you tell by the dragon on his sleeve? God, he's beautiful. I just love him."

The painting will never fade, she said, because it's made with egg tempera.

"What's the—what's it called?" Robert said—"the thing that fixes it all together?"

"The mordant," Millie answered. "You crack the egg and let the white part drip. Then you add vodka. That's the best mordant."

She has made 25 icons. She gave some to friends. Others hang on the wall at St. Paul's Episcopal Church on Abercorn and 34th streets. She gave another one to her gynecologist.

She smiled.

"The virgin and the baby," she said.

The night's movie follows dinner.

It's not that either Robert or Millie would mind company in the cozy corner room of Robert's comfortable home.

"It's just that not everyone shares our taste," Robert said. "We like French movies, Japanese, Indian. We loved *Gate of Hell*, right, Millie? It's one of our favorites, made by moonlight. You kind of live and suffer by the pace of it. Oh, and *House of Flying Daggers*."

"Amazing color," Millie remembered.

The most recent movie they watched was *Nayak: The Hero* by one of their favorite directors, Satyajit Ray. "We've watched about seven of his movies," Robert said. It's about a Bengali film star riding a train, meditating on the dim prospects of his pending film.

Not a lot happens, I commented afterward.

"True, but his films are always beautiful," Millie said.

But about your birthday, I segued, changing the subject, the one where you turn 100.

"You just wake up every morning," Millie said with the slightest smile. That's all she said.

Before long, movie night between a couple of old friends who happen to be neighbors was over. Robert hugged her goodbye, walked her to the door and watched her get home.

7/20/19

5 / Twyla Royal, Jean Crumrine, Bradley's Lock and Key

I knew the key to my truck was looking a little wavy and could probably snap in two any minute. But I've always believed, "If it ain't broke, don't fix it." Mistake No. 1.

(Here's mistake No. IA: If your steering wheel locks, twisting the ignition key as hard as you can does not always help.)

And another thing: Common sense says never load manure into a truck parked in a bog of muck after the heaviest rain in a year. But life's a gamble. It's spring; I need the stuff for my garden. I've driven in snow; I know what to do. Mistake No. 2. At least it wasn't 6 degrees.

And because bad things happen in threes, how could I be surprised when, after calling Bradley's Lock and Key to come and get the two parts of the key to make it whole again (Hey, the man is not named Houdini Bradley for nothing), we return to my car to find both front doors locked. In their excitement, the two enclosed dogs stepped on the buttons, a feature of my 1992 Isuzu truck.

One window was open slightly but not enough for my hefty arm to bend through—or the even heftier arm of the man-from-Bradley's. But like an angel from above, Twyla Royal, the trim and agreeable owner of Victory Feed and Seed, had just pulled up to feed her two horses, Velvet and Jessie. Jessie's the Premarin-baby she rescued from Canada.

We managed to open the car, relieved the broken key could be retrieved from the ignition. Victory No. 1.

Then everyone left—the man-from-Bradley's who left to make a new key, the other woman feeding her horse, and Twyla, but not before trying three times to pull my truck.

There I was, all alone. On twenty acres of pasture, gardens, barns, chickens, piles of manure and five or six pieces of earth-moving equipment poised to work on the Truman Parkway. Before, when we visited to get manure for our gardens, we would hear the sound of guns from the Forest City Gun Club; now it's the sound of construction trucks grinding in reverse.

All alone. With two agitated dogs, one blind pony, one billy goat named Charlotte sitting on a scrap of tin, six horses, five peacocks (crying what sounds like "help, help, help, help") and a pesky and slightly disturbing wind that wouldn't quit.

All alone. Except for Jean Crumrine, 87, owner of the property, the stables, the pastures and one of the best gardens in town. Crumrine broke my reverie, squeezing through the fence, her glasses dangling from a shirt button—not around her neck ("they get in my way weeding the other way")—telling me if I happened to see her grandchildren to say she'd gone off to get groceries.

Crumrine, wearing blue Keds, bought the property some 40 years ago—before The Landings, before the Weatherwood housing development, before the Truman Parkway gouged through the trees, the creeks, the open land.

"It's a high wind, isn't it?" she said. "When you stand here, you can hear the soughing of the pine trees."

Soughing? I asked.

"It's poetic. It means the wind through the pine needles," she explained. "Looks like winter's over. Once the pecan trees leaf out, the cold's past. Those trees are plagued with mistletoe. Mistletoe won't move in on a healthy tree. They were old 40 years ago."

Crumrine learned about nature from her father, who worked as a railroad mechanic ("but he hated it; he was a gardener. I'd go ahead of him and turn the potato vines so he could cut the weeds"). She continues to learn about nature by reading.

"But I read novels when growing up," she said. "I'd wait for Daddy to pick me up in front of the library after I got out of the 38th

Street school."

She was raised in the Ogeechee area. Every fall they'd go chinquapin hunting ("It's kin to the chestnut, has the same burr").

"Look at that peacock," she said as he hopped on her picnic table. "He knows he's beautiful. Isn't that the most beautiful blue ever invented? He thinks my front deck is a parade ground. When he sits on the fence, his tail barely touches the ground. But I can't stand the white feathered peacock. I'd like to lock him up so he can't breathe."

She got her first peacock when he wandered up from the woods. Then one Christmas, "the boys and girls who kept their horses here" bought her a peahen. At one time she had 25. Once a county sheriff complained, "Ms. Crumrine, your peacocks are stopping traffic on Ferguson Avenue."

For the next 30 minutes, Ms. Crumrine showed me her double flowering peach trees, a variety of Indian spinach growing in her Quonset hut/greenhouse with leaves bigger than my hand, the sprigs of her goldenrain tree that has pink seed pods and yellow blooms, the 15-year-old Valencia orange tree, her Lady English peas, her herb garden of oregano, sage and thyme that's grown in the ends of drain pipes so she doesn't have to bend down.

But then she was off to get groceries. She and her grandchildren were going to make challah, a traditional Jewish egg bread she read about once.

Before I could even find a peacock feather, the man-from-Bradley's returned with a new and sturdy key. With several pieces of 2-by-4 under my tires, I gunned the motor and emerged from the muck. Let the day begin.

7/6/15

6 / *Two columns about James Alan McPherson, the first African American to win the Pulitzer Prize for Fiction*

We live in a class-conscious, color-divisive world. We don't want to admit it, but we do. We know our own kind best. Or we think we do. Catholic, Jewish, country, suburban, urban, gay, rich African-Americans, poor African-Americans. We may go to the same schools, shop at the same supermarkets, share the same streets. But we don't have a clue what goes on behind the public facade, the front door.

To hide this ignorance, we rely on stereotypes. That way we can concentrate on the differences instead of the similarities. And there are differences. There are always differences. Between the classes, the ethnic groups, the races. But in the end, we all have the same hassles—how to fit into a community, how to feel good about ourselves, how to do the right thing.

What class you're born into—how much money you have—is huge. So is race. But in the end, the biggest struggle is how to be a good human being.

James Alan McPherson knows that. He's lived it. He's fought it. He's experienced it. He knows about stereotypes. And what happens when you go beyond them. McPherson grew up in Savannah, on Waldburg Street for a while, then 44th Street and Burroughs Street. He grew up poor. His father was an electrical contractor but had trouble with the bottle. He went to segregated schools. In 1961, he graduated from Beach High.

Between going to Morris Brown College, a historically Black liberal arts school in Atlanta, and working during the summer as a waiter on the Great Northern Railway, McPherson got a taste for more. He got into Harvard University and graduated with a law degree. But he didn't want to be a lawyer. He only wanted to understand the law. He wanted to be a writer.

After living in Atlanta; Baltimore; Cambridge; Santa Cruz and Berkeley, California; Rhode Island; Charlottesville, Virginia; and New Haven, Connecticut, McPherson ended up in Iowa City, where he enrolled in the MFA program in the Iowa Writers' Workshop. Now he teaches there. For the past semester or two, he has been the acting director of the program. He also lived in Japan for several years. His memoirs are filled with stories and lessons from other cultures. In between degrees and working on the railroad, he was a lecturer in Japan. He spent years in Baltimore, where, as the owner of a house with deep connections to the people he rented to, he based many of his short stories and much of his ruminations in *Crabcakes: a Memoir.*

Because he read as a child, because he was curious, observant, open and willing to try something he wasn't trained to do, he always wrote stories and submitted them to a creative writing contest sponsored by *Reader's Digest*. Once, he won first prize and got published in *The Atlantic*.

In 1969, McPherson published *Hue and Cry: Stories*, his first book of short stories. In 1977, he published his second, *Elbow Room*, twelve stories about people—some white, mostly black—who are trying to escape racial and sexual stereotypes, characters people like me have to read about to know about.

Then, in 1978, after *Elbow Room*, this graduate of Beach High School—a segregated school in a segregated city in the segregated South—became the first African-American to win the Pulitzer Prize for Fiction, two years after Saul Bellow, two years before Norman Mailer.

A few years later, he received a MacArthur Fellowship awarded to 41 talented U.S. citizens and residents that year. The award carries no strings, only time to think, read, create—or do nothing. He received

$36,800 for each of the next five years or $184,000.

In one interview I read about McPherson, written by Emma Edmunds, he said, "In Savannah, we lived in shacks. We lived in places where if your hand got out at night, a rat would get it. I used to see my father on street corners and run the other way."

Maybe you've heard of Mr. McPherson. I hadn't. Maybe the folks at the Chatham County Board of Education have heard of him—or the staff at Beach High School. I don't know.

I learned about him in a very offhand way from someone I was playing tennis with, also a graduate of Beach. I went to the public library and found his books. *Elbow Room* was in paperback. It was ragged. The first 15 pages were missing.

The rest—*A Region Not Home: Reflections from Exile, Hue and Cry, Crabcakes* and a book about the railroad in American culture—were in better shape.

When I reached McPherson at his Iowa City home, he spoke more fondly of his years at Beach than his time in Savannah.

"The teachers went up North every summer to get more training," he said. "They were well-educated. On Saturdays, they held classes at their homes. They cared about the children."

Which is interesting because, when asked, McPherson said he considers himself more a teacher than a writer. Not a bad combination.

9/7/05

—

McPherson dies
at 73

It's one thing to read the words and stories and meditations of James Alan McPherson. And then, after a while, to pull down the books from the shelves and reread them, because the narrative is not always clear (which is a good thing), the meanings (and timelines) are multiple, the characters (and the narrator) complex.

It's quite another thing altogether to speak with his sister, Mary McPherson. She lives outside Charleston, South Carolina. Mary is one of many relatives and friends who planned yesterday's memorial service at their childhood church, St. Philip Monumental AME, on Jefferson Street. McPherson died July 27 in Iowa City. He was 72.

McPherson, a graduate of Beach High School, may well go down as one of Savannah's finest and least-known writers. He is a Pulitzer Prize-winner in fiction (the first Black person to win in that category), an early recipient of a MacArthur Fellowship and a beloved professor at the respected Iowa Writers' Workshop, in Iowa City.

Saturday's service was not the only celebration of McPherson's life. After his death, the University of Iowa rented the Englert Theatre, in Iowa City. Two hundred colleagues, students and friends crowded together to remember someone they called the moral center and backbone of the Iowa Writers' Workshop. That same day, there was a memorial service at the nearby Trinity Episcopal Church.

According to Mary, one year older than McPherson, she and her siblings left Savannah as soon as they could. "In the early 1960s, opportunities for African-Americans were very, very limited," she said. "Sometimes I look at the raw talent that got away and think: What a shame."

Her brother Richard joined the military. When he finished his term, he worked as an aircraft mechanic with Delta Air Lines in Atlanta. Mary became a corporate librarian and worked in the Northeast for forty years.

Before McPherson left Savannah, he found a home at the Carnegie Library on East Henry Street, a branch of Savannah's Live Oak Public Libraries that has deep roots in the African-American community.

"At first the words without pictures were a mystery," he said in an earlier interview. "But then suddenly they all began to march across the page. They gave up their secret meanings, spoke of other worlds, made me know that pain was a part of other people's lives. After a while I could read faster and faster and faster. After a while I no longer believed in the world in which I lived. I love the colored branch of the Carnegie Public Library."

McPherson's daughter, Rachel, wanted the Savannah memorial to be at the library. But when she found it seated only 75, they moved the service to the church.

"I remember he always read a lot," said Mary. "He would write poems, too. He was like a god in Iowa. People were always coming around, making special noises. When I visited I would have to say, 'Back off. I'm here to see Junior.'"

McPherson kept in close touch with his family. In the last five years, Mary would visit every three months or so. The siblings spoke on the phone two or three times a week. But he had put down deep roots in Iowa.

"One Thanksgiving I decided to go visit," Mary said. "I was all set to cook. Then I noticed a sign he had put up: 'Any student who can't go home please come to my house.' He cooked everything."

At the Iowa City memorial, writer ZZ Packer recalled how McPherson would invite students to his house and lend them books, maybe give them some crab cakes—and sometimes, "if you're real good friends, some bourbon." During one particular visit to Iowa, Mary suggested the two of them visit Savannah.

"Believe it or not, he really wanted to visit. There were people who wanted to bring him there. But by then he had fallen a few times. His mobility was not good. Then he was afraid people might have expected more from him than he could deliver. It just wasn't meant to be.

"While we were considering it, Jim turned to me and said, 'How should I go back? Dead?' I said, 'What? We're not talking about death.' That's when he said, 'I'm just kidding, Mary.'"

When Mary decided to move back South, she considered Savannah. But everything was too expensive. "I came and drove around the old neighborhoods," she said. "Every place I used to live, they had torn down our home. My father's house on Florance Street between 39th and 40th streets was a vacant lot. It was the only house that was missing. It was like they just didn't want us here."

Her brother, she said, "would be appalled at all the fuss we are making. He was so gentle and humble. After he got the Pulitzer, he wanted to run into the woods and hide. He's a very low-key, thoughtful person. Everything he did was from the heart."

9/11/16

7 / *The magic of Sandy West and the number 108*

I never heard Sandy West say she wanted to live to 95 or 100 or 105. If you mentioned any of those numbers she'd turn her head and shrug. She'd wave her graceful hand, her long, tapered fingers, nails frequently painted blue, and say, "Ridiculous" or "Don't tell anyone." Sandy, whose parents passed away much younger than she, lived for the moment. She lived in the moment.

And yet you have to wonder: how was it that two hours into her 108th birthday in the wee hours of the morning this woman who loved to keep people guessing, who appreciated symmetry and the unknown quietly chose this number at which to peacefully die—no muss, no fuss, her earthly "thinking tours" (the term she used for planning her next shenanigan, her next crusade) put to rest. If she were alive, she would say something else was going on for that to happen. She'd point to Hermes, that trickster of a god who showed up at the oddest of times in Sandy's life.

She had it made, you might think. Why bother fighting with the state, confronting the Department of Natural Resources, squabbling with people who wanted her to leave the island before she was ready, standing up to people who preferred she sell the island for big bucks. Relax, lighten up, kick back. Can't you just pretend to be interested, pleaded her lawyer who had been contacted by Aristotle Onassis, an interested buyer, "so I can meet Jackie Kennedy?"

How many people at age 65 have the wherewithal, the gumption, to negotiate their way to a bargain sale with the bureaucrats of the state of Georgia for the future of Ossabaw Island? This after Chatham County hiked her taxes up to a prohibitive amount on an island with no police services, no highway maintenance, no fire department, no school taxes.

This is when it helps to be friends with then-governor Jimmy Carter. Carter—along with another Georgia governor, George Busbee—understood Sandy unlike the state's actuaries who talked right in front of her—"as if I were so old I couldn't hear them"—figuring out how long she might live and what they could do to gobble up the island for themselves. Well, she fooled them. Carter, that beautiful iconoclast of a man, a nonconformist, like Sandy, understood the importance of keeping something wild and untamed.

In her way she was wild and untamed as well. I'm sure her mother did not bring her up to make Ossabaw her home for so long. From the oil painting of Sandy and her brother and all the accoutrements of the rich I'm not sure she would have approved of Sandy's frayed jeans, her scruffy Keds (a style preferred by our new vice-president, Kamala Harris), her occasionally salty language or one of her favorite t-shirts that read, "Life is a Hoax," although maybe she would. Sandy was fond of quoting her mother. "If someone called and she didn't want to speak to them she'd say, 'Tell them I have a bone in my leg.'"

I would not put it past Sandy, who paid attention to numbers and what they meant, to know that 108 has long been considered a sacred number in Hinduism and yoga. Mathematicians view 108 as a number that connects the sun, the moon and the earth. Mystics claim the number represents a key to our own intuition and high aspects of our being. Pranayama—or yoga breathing—are often repeated cycles in sequences of 108. The same with sun salutations, which are completed in nine rounds of the 12 postures. When multiplied they add up to 108.

Leonardo Fibonacci, who taught us about the golden ratio, or the spiral arrangement of leaves of petals, said the number 108 represents the wholeness of existence. Once a month the distance between the earth and the sun is 108 times the diameter of the sun. The Yoga Institute says when the number 108 appears in our life it may mean that we are about to attain a long-desired goal or achievement.

Did Sandy know there are 108 hand-stitched stiches in a Major League Baseball? Maybe. There was no second-guessing Eleanor "Sandy" Torrey West. You never knew what she'd say. We thought she'd live forever.

But now is when things get real. In the spring of 2020 with the near passage of HB 906 we barely escaped legislation that would privatize historic structures and allow the state to sell up to and including 15 acres of Heritage Preserve property, such as Ossabaw—just the thing Sandy warned us about. The bill is going to come up again; count on it.

As Sandy exhorted us time and again, we have to be in her army. We have to be her army. Now it's our time to step up to protect Ossabaw and other coastal islands. She did her part. Now it's our turn.

1/24/21

8 / Jack Leigh

Most people who know Jack Leigh associate him with photography, especially after his shot of the Bird Girl statue became so closely bound to *Midnight in the Garden of Good and Evil.*

His is a world of black and white. Fog-shrouded marshes. Creeks at low tide. Shrimpers making a wide arc with their nets. Afternoon checker games in the neighborhood.

The shots are austere and ascetic. There's a beauty to their isolation, a stillness to their subject matter. But few people, unless they grew up with him, know of Leigh's passion for sports, not the couch potato variety, but the drive that makes a person get out and practice, then compete. In his youth, the tall and rangy Leigh captained football and basketball teams, played in the Municipal League, wore the black-and-orange striped jersey of Savannah's erstwhile Tigers' Club, which met in Daffin Park.

In the late '50s, when Mickey Mantle and the rest of the New York Yankees stopped off for an exhibition game with the Red Legs team in Grayson Stadium, Leigh pulled on his Little League uniform and headed for the ballpark.

So before the 1996 Olympics, when officials asked him to photograph Grayson Stadium as a way to woo the women's softball competition to Savannah, he accepted. But in typical Leigh fashion, not without doing lots of research.

In the same way he would spend two years on the Ogeechee River choosing his shots, meeting the local people, attending every fried-red-bream dinner he could, Leigh, 55, studied the stadium. That's when he learned that Babe Ruth played in the Victory Drive park, as did

"Shoeless Joe" Jackson.

"Jackson enjoyed his time here so much—this was about 1907 or '06—that he returned and opened a dry-cleaning business, right here, right next to my studio," Leigh said, his blue eyes wide with excitement at the notion.

Savannah didn't win the softball venue because politics got in the way, Leigh said. But the city did get a great shot of Grayson.

And that's how Leigh hooked up with Mike Kasino of today's Sand Gnats organization.

New to town, Kasino was knocked out by the black-and-white photograph. It spoke volumes of memories and emotions to him. He sought out Leigh to learn more about the stadium and the old days of Savannah. The two became fast friends. That friendship is how the famed photographer happened to find himself standing on the pitcher's mound last Thursday night before the first game of the season.

"When I got sick back in December," Leigh said of his fight with cancer, "right off the bat, Mike said, 'I want you to throw out the first ball.' He said it would be a goal for me and an honor for them. It was such a wonderful gesture—and is so much a part of my day-to-day on-goingness."

On Thursday night, the man who always wanted to be an artist but never could in high school "because back then only girls took art classes," arrived at 5:45 wearing his maroon-and-green silk Sand Gnats jacket and trademark Levi's.

Tears weren't streaming down his face—which is how he described starting work on his first book project, heading out in a bateau early in the morning, no longer painting houses for a living or serving drinks as a bartender, knowing he had found his life's work— but Leigh, whose spirit lives in the marsh, the fog, the cotton fields— looked at the stadium, witnessed the fans lining up for tickets and appeared happy, almost blissful.

Blissful as in knowing when to click the shutter and get the perfect shot—the microsecond, the blink-of-an-eye moment, the focus required to understand an aesthetic moment. He seemed to relish the occasion.

No longer able to work independently, the man who loved the

challenge of hanging off a shrimp boat and changing lenses in the wind, arrived with a coterie of longtime friends, family members and assistants for physical and moral support.

These days, when he's well, when he's energized, Leigh is either fooling around with a Polaroid or, with the help of gallery employees Susan Laney and Ben Beasley, continuing to document the evolution of the Telfair Museum's Jepson Center.

"It's a new thing for me, working with people," he said. "But when you get sick like this, you can either think it's the most tragic thing that ever happened or you can rise to another profound level of relationship.

"As horrible as this illness is—and there are days when I wonder whether I can make it—the other levels have made me happier than I've ever been in life. Because when all barriers are down—and believe me, they've been down—you know you're surrounded by love and community, which is the way we were meant to live, heart to heart, mind to mind, soul to soul. Nothing else really matters."

Except, perhaps, for making that throw to the catcher and presenting a decent showing on opening day.

"I'm feeling good," he said, after taking a couple dozen practice throws in front of the visitor's dugout. "It's a beautiful night at the ballpark."

Then, right on cue, after the crowd sang the national anthem and Mayor Otis Johnson said a few words, Leigh walked to the mound and fired a strike.

"Right down the middle," he said afterwards, pumping his arm and grinning at his supporters in the stands.

"All that training paid off, baby."

4/11/04

9 / *Scott Stanton*
(aka Panhandle Slim)

All his life people have been telling Scott Stanton to get a real job, to grow up. It's not that he was a slacker; he wasn't. At 20 he was a professional skateboarder. Think that doesn't translate into big bucks? Think again. In three years he made enough money to put himself through college. Before he was 23 he had traveled to Europe, Australia, Japan, Mexico and Canada. Not bad for doing a few crazy tricks on a wooden board with wheels on it. Not bad for following his passion. He got paid for his antics, for creating something new every time he flew into the air like some berserk creative ballerina with a new maneuver to show off. He got paid for allowing some big company to paint his name on a board and giving him a few bucks every time one sold.

Then the whole thing got too big. It spiraled out of control. Skateboarding became a business. He became a commodity. He could spot the money people a mile away. The passion dimmed. He turned to music, to a band he formed with his wife, Tracy, while going to the University of Florida, in Gainesville. They called themselves the Causey Way. Compared to the skateboard crowd, traveling with a band seemed like hanging out with the Mouseketeers.

By his mid-20s, living in Kalamazoo, Michigan, where his wife got a job teaching art at Kalamazoo College, Scott tried a more traditional approach. He became a substitute teacher in a local high school. Not exciting, that. Just a job, like everyone told him he should get. He wasn't averse to manual labor either; he painted houses, worked on a tree farm and clerked in a paint store.

Then something broke through. An idea. A new path. He was visiting a folk art gallery in Grand Rapids where he saw a Howard Finster-like painting he coveted. Only he couldn't afford it. He and Tracy had a young son and just enough money to get by. That's when Scott thought, "I can do that." So he did. He had always doodled. He had always sketched. And he was good with tools. He got a hold of a jigsaw and cut a panel from some old wood lying around, and he started drawing. His first three images were Dolly Parton, Jimmy Carter and Malcolm X.

He had stumbled upon a new passion. The former skateboarder from the Florida Panhandle had a new direction. And a new moniker: Panhandle Slim.

Scott kept at it. Never a good student in high school, he discovered his curiosity—intellectual curiosity—in college. Through his major in sociology and social work at the University of West Florida, he started reading more. He started thinking about words and how they would work with pictures. And then along came the World Wide Web. When friends told him he should sell his paintings on eBay, Scott laughed. He told them they had lost their mind. The first one—the Dukes of Hazzard—sold for $10. "I couldn't believe it," he said. "It was good lunch money."

Then Facebook came along. He started posting images. People started contacting him, and he'd ship the paintings out. For a while he numbered them. He stopped at 1,000 in 2006. When the shipping got to be too much of a logistical factor, he quit. Now he just paints. You'll know his paintings; they're everywhere. Bright colors, primitive images, single quotes from people like Maya Angelou and Jimmy Carter.

The couple moved to Savannah eight years ago when Tracy got a job at SCAD. For a while Scott had shows at the old Hang Fire bar. They'd sell "from $45 to a couple hundred. I'd tell people to name a price, but they're not comfortable with that." Now, instead of shipping the paintings, he'll tell potential buyers to drop the money through the mail slot of his house and pick up the work in his carport.

A few years ago he hooked up with a couple of savvy community activists who spotted the positive messages and the political commentary on his paintings and wanted to help spread the word. Now Beverlee Trotter, of Savannah Youth City, and Erika Hardnett, from Agape Empowerment Ministries, find walls on barbershops, carwashes, confectionary stores. Scott's pal Sebastian Edwards hangs them.

"It's become a community thing," Scott said. "When we start to screw them into concrete walls, people come out to see what's going on. It reminds me of the old days when people would sit outside and talk."

Most days, Scott, wearing a trademark Panama hat and maybe a short-sleeved checked cotton shirt, sets up in a restaurant (preferably one with Muzak) with his spiral notebook, the newspaper and his son, Tex. While Tex studies maps and birds on his laptop, Scott scouts around for ideas. He likes to do at least one painting a day.

He's done gallery shows, but the whole thing with white walls and owners doesn't appeal to him. He'd rather look around for sites, load up his van, announce where he'll be and just show up. At the end of the day, it's one-on-one. Once he drove out to California with his work. He'd go into a restaurant and start talking to the owner before popping the question, "Do you like art?"

"Keeps it interesting," he said. "Art and money are strange things. We're all artists. When it stops feeling good, I'll do something else. I always wanted a lawn business."

8/14/16

10 / *Remembering Ed Fletcher (aka Duke Bootee)*

Celebrities abound. They're everywhere. We just don't always know or see them. Did I ever run into Sandra Bullock in the super market or the bank? No. But I did pass her beach house on the north end of Tybee Island (it had a long walkway over the dunes), the one that just sold for $4.2 million.

Then there was that meet-and-greet cocktail party at Rosemary Daniell's house when she lived on Habersham Street. Rosemary, a productive writer, a generous writing coach and an openhanded connector of people was the consummate host. I'm standing there, new in town, feeling somewhat awkward in a room of people I don't know, holding a drink, when a tallish, unpretentious man approached our group. We introduced ourselves, then he said, "Hi, I'm Pat Conroy." Sure, I thought. And I'm Joyce Carol Oates.

Seconds later, Rosemary joins our group and says, "Pat! Glad you could make it."

Late to the party, that's me. Which is how I felt when I met and learned about Ed Fletcher, who passed away a few weeks ago from heart failure. This long-time music producer and his wife Rosita had just moved to town after taking a trip to Key West in the early 90's from their home in New Jersey. They had stopped along the way in Savannah, long enough for them to decide to rent a place and move here. Someone thought we should meet. They were renting a small garage apartment in Ardsley Park so one Sunday I went over for a chit-chat. They seemed nice. Rosita was gracious, Ed electric, a storyteller, a bit cantankerous. It was a nice combo. They loved going to the beach early in the morning. He said he liked to play tennis. I said, "Let's play sometime."

After they rented a house on my street in Parkside, we started spontaneously meeting early in the morning to walk around the park. We talked about the regulars who were there every day. We shared dreams we'd had the night before. We got chummy and casual the way new neighbors in your immediate vicinity will do. I'd walk my dogs past his house and see him on his front porch using his battery-powered toothbrush. We'd wave. He'd ask for the name of an electrician, a plumber, a banker, a lawyer. When his children and grandchildren visited from up north, they invited us to their backyard for barbecue. We reciprocated.

I still wasn't quite sure what he did, maybe something in music except he said he had been a teacher in New Jersey so I was a little confused. There just wasn't enough time for each of us to go into detail. At a certain age, we have a lot of gaps to fill, many decades. He showed me a studio he fixed up behind his house. We never went in. We talked grandchildren. We talked life. After he started teaching at Savannah State University, we talked millennials, Gen Xers, Gen Yers, the MTV generation, the way people our age will do, envious of their skills in technology yet critical of them too. Put the phone down (but first explain how to send a message). Forget about social media for a second.

He was also a snappy dresser, that's for sure, his dreads tucked under some kind of knitted Jamaican hat or piled into a bun atop his head, never wearing the same thing twice at art openings around town, never showing up without a hand-chewed cigar he never lit. He had attitude; I just wasn't sure what it was.

He liked to garden. When they bought a house in Gordonston he couldn't wait to show me what he had done with the backyard. It was a little neater than I prefer but I loved his enthusiasm. He had plans. By this time they had two more grandchildren.

It was during one of these gatherings that I mentioned to someone in her 30s, who worked at the Sentient Bean, I wasn't really clear on who Ed Fletcher was. She stopped me in mid-sentence. "You're kidding." Not really. "You mean you never heard 'The Message'?" Nope. "The song he did with Grandmaster Flash? One of the first rap songs to focus on social commentary, good enough to get into the Library of Congress? I know you know it.

I didn't.

Turns out this middle-class son of educators (a principal and a teacher), this prolific rap music producer who preferred his gardens organized and filled with color, whose message to his students was to take care of business (and their teeth), who liked a home filled with local art (and an upright tuned piano), who like me had fantasies of playing killer tennis, was able to turn his prescient and bold eye on life in the city before anyone else in the hip hop world.

And then to turn all this into a college class called "Critical Thinking." Those lucky Savannah State University students. They won't forget the irascible, questioning, complicated Ed Fletcher. Neither will the rest of us.

1/31/21

WORTHY THINGS TO DO DURING THE PANDEMIC

Find and change all passwords.
Resist getting a third dog (when the 12-year-old
just won't play with the 1-year old).
Read the one hundred twenty-five-page
    Medicare & You 2021 handbook.
Get to the bottom of this no-sound-on-your-laptop
    business.
Gather all your stamps in one location.
Dust (power wash?) the top of your ceiling fans.
Throw away bank statements from 1993.
Learn the difference between your IRA and
    your regular account.
Nip this recent excessive use of exclamation marks
in the bud.
Figure out how radios work.
Give up on the French thing; not going to happen.
Give up plastic.
Get the multiple-keys situation resolved.
Explain photosynthesis in 25 words or less.

THE VIRUS

[IN CHRONOLOGICAL ORDER]

1 / *Clean fingernails*
(before we took
the virus seriously)

I don't know about other gardeners, but since the coronavirus has started to take over our lives, my fingernails have never been cleaner. I no longer have to hide my fingers in my lap—or tuck them under a shirt sleeve—when I go out in public. My computer keyboard looks pretty good, too. The "L" no longer sticks. Same with the "G." What a concept: washing away the dirt and/or the crumbs before opening the lid and striking a key. Sometimes I look down and don't even know whose hands these nails belong to. My sink has never been emptier of dirty dishes, either. I knew there was a reason to hand-wash instead of filling up the dishwasher (when you never can be sure if the dishes have been washed or not). Dish detergent counts as a hand sanitizer, doesn't it? Sort of? Just when it's become acceptable for women to shake hands like all the other adults (make that men) in the room, we can't. Not fair. Yes, a fist bump feels cool and an elbow bump looks hip but, hey, can we agree both lack a certain elegance?

Since one of the things we're not supposed to do in this hyper-vig-ilant time is use the gasoline pump without putting on latex gloves and/or taking time to wipe off the pumps, maybe it's time to bring back the old-fashioned service stations (emphasis on service, on hu-man contact). Some old-timers call them filling stations. I always liked that phrase, though I never used it. This is where attendants (some-times called gas jockeys) pumped the gas for us while we stayed in the car and stared out the window. No cell phones back then. They would wipe your windows, check your tires and sometimes give you a free prize with a fill-up. Can I get an "Amen"? Those were the days we could roll down the window (well, some of us can still) and say, "Fill 'er up!" I'm sure you've seen that in old movies. New Jersey knows all about this. This prescient, farsighted state banned self-service in 1949. (OK, so it probably had something to do with kickbacks for certain unions; still, it feels pretty good—and as it happens it's hygienic—to have someone else pump your gas.) Take that, you-think-you're-so-smart California! Parts of Oregon did the same thing. By the way, remember when it wasn't kosher for women to fill their own gas tanks? Think I'm making this up? Not.

Lots to think and worry about these days—and not just cancelling trips to China or Italy. Time to pump up the garlic consumption. But wait! You wouldn't believe how much of our garlic comes from China. Check the label. Another supply chain lost to the virus. (Did you ever imagine using the words "supply chain" in a sentence?) Fortunately, my winter crop is looking good. I dug up a bulb the other day just to check on its progress; it's big but not big enough. Patience. They're homegrown but garlic requires constant weeding, which leads to more handwashing. Win-win.

It's time to pump up consumption of ginger, cinnamon and turmeric, too. But we've always done that, right? Time to focus on eating raw veggies. Because of this wacko weather, I've got a plethora of sugar snap peas that I planted two months earlier than usual, just on a wild bet the warm weather would hold. It did, too. Usually I don't plant them until the middle of January. The problem with planting them early is the possibility of an overnight freeze just when they're starting to bud out. I've lost a few sprouts from a cold night or two but nothing too serious. The peas are starting to produce. Glory be. Crunch, crunch, snap, snap. But as many as I have, I wish I had ten times more. I ran out of space. Time to create more space. Which means more digging, the natural antidepressant, Prozac without side effects, serotonin on demand. We must never forget the efficacy of soil microbes.

In the meantime, there's always chicken soup, the Jewish cure, the original penicillin. Do not underestimate the tried and true.

2 / So much to worry about (will I be the next one?)

Oh my, so much to worry about. Even if you weren't in the designated pandemic danger zone of "the elderly." Did I just touch the knob of my front door? Could the postal carrier have sneezed on it? Must wash hands now! What about the mail he or she dropped through the slot? We know how many people must have handled that. Then there's that $20 bill I just fished out of my wallet to pay for gas. That was stupid. Who knows how many people have TOUCHED that particular bill, SICK people who haven't been tested, who don't know they are sick? (And what's this urgent propensity toward using CAPITAL LETTERS to MAKE A POINT?).

Anyway, we may launder money but we never clean it. I haven't seen anyone warn us about moving to credit cards. I love cash. In and out. No record. Easy peasy. Am I willing to wear gloves for that love?

Quick: Find the soap. Good business to be in these days: soap. Same thing with home cleaning appliances such as vacuum cleaners. (Wonder if any are manufactured in the United States or do they all come from China?). Almost as good a business as lawyers specializing in divorce. All this close contact, you know, working at home, staying home, getting in one another's lane. The divorce rate in China, I read, is up.

But it's mostly about soap.

"Out, damned spot!"

Surely anyone who read *Macbeth* in 10th grade English (or took

Shakespeare with Professor Arthos at the University of Michigan) must be saying those words again and again, simultaneously recalling Lady Macbeth's guilt and near insanity after she talked her husband into doing the killing. You nailed it, Shakespeare.

Oh, for the days when all we had to worry about were eggs. Is it safe to eat more than one a day? When we talked about the efficacy of walking versus running, the danger of forgetting to apply sunscreen, the stupidity of putting off the shingles vaccine. Is it that important to only eat organic fruits and vegetables? All of that seems irrelevant. At this point it doesn't matter how much we floss, how much water we drink, whether or not we touch our faces, how fast we pay off our mortgages.

Now there's only one big question behind every news cycle, each caveat. There's only one biggie: Will I be the one who gets "it"? Will I be in the path of those toxic droplets? In short, will I die?

The near insanity of Lady Macbeth. That's how we feel. Each day brings a new tidbit, a new crumb of craziness. How about the folks in prison? Millions of them. (P.S.: Prisons are moneymakers for small towns.) No social distancing there. No hand sanitizers, either. Not because they aren't available. Not because the imprisoned can't afford them. The real reason? Because they contain alcohol. Can't trust them not to drink it. Yum. What about people who work in prisons and return home after work? I doubt they're thinking about touching door knobs, coffee pots, television remotes, their cell phones.

I remember the anthrax scare of the early '90s. For years every bit of mail that came into the newsroom had to be opened before it got to us reporters. This seems different.

Spam, on the other hand, does not change. Take the cry for "Virus blockers." The term has taken on a new meaning. The inconsequential daily emails keep on coming—from Uncle Jim's Worm Farm, Compressa Socks, Choice Home Warranty—as if nothing has changed. "Same as it ever was, same as it ever was," says the Talking Heads, another line that reverberates.

Except it's not. Everything is taking on new meaning. Old movies where we see people standing too close together and shaking hands. New (newish) movies such as "Contagion," made in 2011, about a global pandemic. Old books like Albert Camus' *The Plague*, unavailable from the library, impossible to find in bookstores. And then Geraldine Brooks' *Year of Wonders*, a doozy of a book I located under the B's (miracle of miracles) on my bookshelf. It's set in 17th-century England and is about a village that quarantines itself against the spread of plague. Sound familiar?

I'm not so sure I'll get to Zach Powers' *100 Things To Do in Savannah Before You Die*. Hmm, not this month. Right now, I don't especially like those words—"before I die." Right now, I'm putting in bush beans, nurturing itty-bitty celery starts, walking my dog Sweetie, expecting the worst, hoping for the best.

3/22/20

3 / *The spring plant swap that wasn't (and we thought we'd be fine come fall)*

Dear People of the Plant Swap,

Remember all those little packets of seeds you got many moons ago? The ones you grabbed, stuck in a bowl, intending to plant but never did because, well, it's spring (or fall) and there's just so much other stuff to do in the yard, in the garden, at the beach? Right now I am looking at about a dozen. I know I have a couple more dozen stashed somewhere else. These on hand include datura (yellow and purple), orange pepperoncini (hot pepper), fire catcher sunflower, lemonade cosmos, jungle parrot (a variety of sweet pepper). Each of the so-called eight tattoo papaya is about the size of a grain of kosher salt.

Someone—you know who you are—carefully and thoughtfully extracted those tiny seeds (not always an easy task) from a host plant at just the right time after the temperatures cooled and the seeds hardened. You inserted them in those tiny plastic bags, neatly printed those names and brought them to our biannual plant swap.

Alas, now in the throes of COVID-19 is the spring you will be able to plant them. Alone. By yourself.

If the plant swap wasn't so popular, so well attended, if there weren't such a crush of people, if we weren't always so happy to see one another, we might consider going ahead with the first-Saturday-in-April schedule. Alas, alack, we cannot. We will have to push the "Pause" button for now. Too many people too close together, too excited to brag about something they had to share, something they just had to have, something they propagated, babied, watched over, something they wanted to give away.

It could be their blooming queen's tears (or billbergia), that uncomplaining bromeliad—so popular at the plant swaps—that just wants to be left alone. "Don't even look at it," I advise people when I see them walking away with armfuls of them from previous swaps. "Don't pay it no mind." Sure enough. After properly ignoring a thick clump I rescued from the lane years ago after someone moved, after forgetting I even had it, this blast of color, fuchsia, purple, red came shooting my way one morning last week.

Then there are the zinnias that came with this note: "First planted in 1942. Share the love."

How about the crocosmia corms? These are a regular every year because they, you know, are famous for never staying in their lane. This batch came with these words (without the warning): "I'm crocosmia. I have a spray of tiny orange flowers and if you cut that off I'll bloom again. Plant me in full sun and I'll be happy."

Oh, so happy. Beware.

Another favorite offering read, "Mystery pepper. Will help make you HOTTER. Likes shade/part sun and sweet whisperings."

At the plant swap that wasn't, we could have expected air potato vines, morning glory seeds, walking iris, obedient plants, papyrus, spiny aloe.

This spring we will have to find another way to show off our garden. I've already been talking to myself. How about those viral banana trees, still putting out bananas! Don't forget the young red cannas. They will never look so good, never stand so strong. What about the evening primrose (oenothera), that pink beauty that some people eschew because of its tendency to spread? I say, bring it on! And oh, is there anything prettier than an early American beautyberry leaf?

Even the lethal prickly pear cactus looks beautiful.

At first, we thought about holding an abbreviated plant swap. Bring what you have to the garden, spread it out on the ground, look around, see if there's anything you might want and then leave. No crowds. That was before the mandatory two-week stay-at-home order that extends until the middle of April.

Right now, when you get tired of organizing your closet, cleaning out your vegetable bin, arranging your books in alphabetical order, learning how to play chess, pick up a shovel, do some digging, plant those seeds and maybe some vegetables, too. It's a perfect time. Then come back for the fall plant swap—first Saturday in October—with some new things to brag about. Me? I'm hoping for big things from my bush beans, pole beans, basil, arugula, sorrel, borage, eggplant and celery.

Heck, I'm still picking the last of a stellar sugar snap season and those reliable collard greens. That's an essential activity, right? Just like going to the grocery store.

3/29/20

4 / *The mercurial March (oh, to say, "now, where was I?")*

At this rate in this stay-at-home business, the woman across the street playing the trumpet should be ready for a little Dizzy Gillespie. (I know I'm ready.) She's getting better. That's impressive. It's not Italians singing arias—or squeezing boxes—from their porches but it is music. These are Richie Havens days. And Nina Simone. And soul singer Bettye LaVette, who never heard of the Beatles' "Blackbird" before she recorded it for a recent album.

The good news is, unlike in the season of hurricanes, we still have electricity. Which means no silence-piercing generators (there's always one in the neighborhood). Bette Midler tweets that New York City is so quiet you can hear the rats having sex.

But wait. There's more good news: all those bikes leaning against garages, tangled up in seasons of jasmine and honeysuckle, are art projects waiting to be freed, waiting to be ridden. Be still my heart: children on bikes. With their parents. Kids with helmets, adults without. People waving as they ride by. The empty streets have never been more conducive to bike riding. People on front porches catching breezes not droplets (will we ever use that word again?). People going out for walks, especially around dinnertime.

Dogs? I'm not so sure how happy they are. The best cartoon I've seen lately had a dog perched on top of some tall kitchen cabinets, looking down at a human and saying, "No! No more walks!"

Eye contact seems to be the thing we crave, if just from a distance.

Which is not to dismiss virtual eye contact. Witness teachers spending hours talking about Google Hangouts, WeChat, Voom, Viber. Not for me, I think. Let me go pick the last of the broccoli, the remaining sugar snap peas. I'd rather stick a sharp object in my eye than come up with one more password, install one more app, listen to one more person ask ever so sweetly, "May I drive?" Yet it's tempting. I give in. I succumb.

And there I am (with a little help from a friend), seeing and talking (with only the slightest delay) to people in my book group. Ah, color me happy. It didn't matter what we were talking about. It was just so grand seeing them. Despite the circumstances, I felt we had a focused, back-and-forth discussion. No getting up for another drink, no talking in small groups, no sneaking a look down at a text, no moving in for another Girl Scout cookie. But was it just two weeks ago we debated getting together, albeit six feet apart? I guess one more app couldn't hurt me.

None of us chose to have this much time at home. Sometimes, I feel guilty for enjoying it so much. How else would we have emptied the pantry, wiped it down, thrown away questionable bags of pasta, found the flaxseed we knew we had, found the lentils, so many lentils—oh, so many lentils. The freezer is next. The last time we went through it was when we were bracing for a hurricane, emptying frozen chunks of mystery food into ice chests.

Very satisfying. Like looking at bush beans push their way to the surface in four days. Like biking over to the Farmers Market 912 Food Truck and finding them nearly sold out (satisfying for them, not for me). Like finding a stash of fresh parsley growing in the East 49th Street lane, with permission from Mary, the gardener, to pick it. Like taking my truck to Mickey, the mechanic, and receiving from Carmelita, the woman who works there a huge bag of lemons, enough to give away to the parsley gardener.

My biggest fear? The worst sign so far? The month of March. It was supposed to come in like a lion, out like a lamb. Like everything else in this wacky world, things did not work out that way. I get the lion part. Going to two funerals at the end of February (that almost counts for March, right?) for two lions: community gardener George Wilson and the irreplaceable Laura Devendorf. And then in the middle of March, the startling death of the inimitable Arnold Tenenbaum, a victim of COVID. Three people I thought would live forever, three warriors, three gentle souls, all with big hearts, big ideas. The rest of March? It did not do what it was supposed to do. And that, my friends, is what has me worried. I think we're in for the long haul. I look forward to the day when I wake up and can say, now where was I? What was I doing?

4/5/20

5 / *Wrangling bamboo and the virus (And now it's Yom Kippur: May you be inscribed in the book of life.)*

Enough already. Enough with the charts, the probabilities, the press conferences, the make-it-yourself masks, the blue gloves, the ventilators, the blame game, the bogus cures, the obfuscation, the sleight of hand, the grandstanding, the firings, the webinaring, the zooming, the grooming (I just read something from a bigwig at Walmart that the chain is showing increased sales of "tops" but not "bottoms" because so many people are videoconferencing from home, so all that matters is what shows above the waist—commerce: on top of things, as usual).

Enough with once-innocent-now-verboten activities like this line, straight out of Michael Cunningham's *The Hours*: "She offers her cheek for a kiss." This about the complex and conflicted Mrs. Dalloway as she sashays onto the street, heading for the flower shop before the big party she will give that night.

Enough with prescient and ironic questions asked every year at this week's Passover Seder, where freedom from slavery is a basic theme: "Why is this night different from all other nights?" (it's a long story, the answer). And plagues? You want to talk plagues? I'll give you a plague.

Not to be forgotten is this pronouncement, which follows the Jewish High Holidays known as Rosh Hashanah (the New Year) and Yom Kippur (the Day of Atonement): "May you be inscribed in the book of life," the idea being that at the end of ten days, the days of repentance, God will have decided who gets to live another year.

We're months before those holidays, but with this kind of familiar question rolling around our brains, it doesn't take much for a person to ask: By the way, Yahweh, was I inscribed last year? Just wondering. Did I pass muster? How am I doing so far this year? Asking for a friend.

Even with proper distancing, constant wiping, endless handwashing, does anyone else feel like we're playing a game of Russian roulette? That just by being alive, we're spinning the cylinder, pointing the gun to our heads, pulling the trigger and hoping for the best?

It's time for a break. And I don't mean another Dilly Bar.

Time to remember Al Kaline, that straight arrow, Baltimore-born, standup guy who roamed center field 22 seasons for the Detroit Tigers. He died this week, the man known as "Mr. Tiger." My cousin Melvin's favorite sportsperson ever. Even his name stands straight up, the A, the K, the two Ls.

Time for a daily bocce ball bout in Forsyth Park (family members only handling the balls).

Time to battle some bamboo, which means time to tuck one's tail, eat some crow and start wrangling, because it was my idea to put it there in the first place, my idea to pull it up from some random field and bring it back home. Be careful, people warned. It's invasive. If it's not the clumping kind (it wasn't), it will take over (it did). You'll rue the day you planted it. No, no, no, I said. I'll keep it under control. I'll watch it. I'll monitor it. It's so elegant, so delicate, those lithe branches catching a breeze, waving so gently. So tropical. So equatorial. It was doing everything I wanted and more.

I marveled at its beauty. OK, it tended to pop up here and there. No problem. I'd reach for my shovel and whack the little uprisings away. *Take that!* I'd say. *I am in control here.*

Nothing stopped it from growing: neither hurricane winds, 100-degree days, overnight frosts. *Go forth*, I'd say. Then I started seeing multiple eruptions. Two here, four there, another six in another corner. Two came up in the chicken coop, reaching to the roof as if they were a support stud. Bamboo, thy name is tenacity.

Time to call a friend. As he traced extensive root perambulations under the yard—alongside a piece of PVC pipe, through the azaleas, near the garage—I started hauling everything into the lane. That's when I must have left the gate to the lane open and gone inside to take a break. That's when I got a call from a neighbor. One of my chickens had flown the coop (except, shh, she doesn't know she can fly; she merely walked into the lane). I scooted out in time to see three shrieking pre-teenage girls on their bikes riding through the lane as if it were a dirt path derby, laughing at another neighbor trying to corral the chicken back into the yard. No easy task.

By the end of the day, the chickens were reunited, the yard was free of bamboo (for now) and I was grateful for the distraction. The job did the trick. All afternoon I was away from news, away from book-of-life issues. In a few months we can start to worry about a hurricane season that's on tap to be above normal. My only question is, which will come back first: the coronavirus or the bamboo?

4/12/20

6 / *Carrying on and finding my joy (When the pandemic meant trading food, making do, la la la)*

So how's your pandemic going?

The question, so oddly phrased but offered with humor, with a smile, floated across the sidewalk from someone on his bike. He was grinning, his cheeks were flushed. He was energized by an early evening ride through the neighborhood on streets with few cars. He was away from the screen. He looked happy.

He caught me off guard. He caught me at a good moment. Homemade rye bread (in exchange for homegrown mustard greens, one fat onion and a big ol' rutabaga) sat on the front porch—next to a brown bag of chocolate-covered Matzo—while homemade collard "stew" (cooked with my homegrown collards) sat on a shelf in the fridge next to homegrown broccoli sprouts (in exchange for homemade gluten-free brownies) to say nothing of home-cooked peanut butter/chocolate rice crispy squares and lemon bars handed over for homemade black bean soup and a few slices of orange-glazed ham (or was it corned beef?).

I'm telling you: food is flying. Consumption of junk food may be on the rise for some, but for people who like to cook, now is the time. Trading is active. Pickled Florida betony roots (yes, those ubiquitous white, square-stemmed, hairy tubers also known as rattlesnake weed are good for something) for baby celery plants. Book delivery from The Book Lady for a check and a handful of the last of the sugar snap peas. Okra seeds from Southern Roots Seeds in exchange for shoveling some compost and sitting (hopefully at the proper distance but who knows?) around a table to shell some peas.

Life is good, I might say to the young man on the bicycle—if I had the nerve, if the whole world wasn't going to hell in a handbasket, if it didn't feel so wrong to feel so good, if so many people weren't scared and dying, if hourly workers didn't have to take a crowded bus to get to work to get a paycheck while I sat home enjoying the luxury of not having to go anywhere, if learning to play an instrument if I wanted to (I don't) was an option, if I wanted to pick up a No. 2 pencil and draw my dog (I might).

If I would answer honestly, I might say: Yes, life is good. It's simpler, less complicated. More streamlined. There's no second-guessing the hours of the library; it's closed. No double-booking lunches or dinners. No forgetting doctor appointments. Even the dreaded April 15 deadline for filing income tax returns has come and gone with approved postponement.

Life was good—until I had to go to Staples to get a printer cartridge, my first outing behind a face mask (I could get used to grocery deliveries; it's kind of fun to see different products. Vanilla yogurt means one thing to me, another to the in-store shopper). Walking into that supply store was my first encounter with paranoia, with fear. *Get me in, get me out*, I am screaming on the inside. This is the kind of soldier I would be if I had been drafted into the Vietnam War. Worried. On edge. Tense. I was filled with emotions I didn't know I had.

Life was good—until I visited my friend Virginia. She's in an assisted living facility. We talked through a closed window, she sitting in her room with a companion, she who doesn't care for television, who likes to be around people, who likes people, me standing outside trying to lead her through a few small hand and arm exercises.

Life is good when I'm in the car, listening to the radio (anything but the news), windows down, arm out, wind blowing, driving anywhere, it doesn't matter. The Savannah National Wildlife Refuge is a good choice. From that perspective everything looks the same. Everything looks as it always did. Is there a pandemic? Life is good when I'm walking my dog Sweetie in the lane and I hear the woodpecker tapping against the tin around the chimney (I want to tell him, "If you want worms, try some wood," but what do I know?), when we run into Tina Turner, the dog on the corner.

Life is good until I return home and hear Lucinda Williams singing, "You took my joy, I want it back. You took my joy. I want it back."

I'm waiting to leave home with purpose, to do what I want when I want, where I want. I'm waiting for the next season of *Ozark*. Until then my job is to find my joy. Today it was bending low to see the miniature heart-shaped leaves of the season's first okra plant. It's miniscule, it's just one, but I'll take it. It's a start.

4/18/20

7 / Something is in the air
(Am I being
careful enough?)

"She offers her cheek for a kiss." She being the beautiful and conflict-ed Clarissa Vaughan who visits the floral shop on some fancy street in Manhattan. Just a brief blip of a moment. Clarissa is giving a par-ty that evening for an author friend with AIDS who may or may not show up. This is from Michael Cunningham's novel *The Hours*.

But in the age of a pandemic, how jarring. How daring. To offer a cheek. For a kiss.

How unsafe. To give a party. With people mingling and intermin-gling. In 2020.

All our reference points are changing. Will we ever look at a towering magnolia tree with those large white blooms so beautiful-ly spaced and think about anything other than proper social distanc-ing? I thought the same thing about the sparsely positioned parsley leaves I was pulling off last night for tabouli. And the way our cat and dog situated themselves on the front porch. All properly spaced from each other.

One day, sure enough, the term "social distancing" will be the an-swer to a board game. For now, it permeates everything we see.

Was it just eight weeks ago we sheepishly offered an elbow instead of a hand or a hug at a neighbor's house, laughing as we extended—of all ridiculous things—that joint between the upper and lower part of the arm, moving all the while in a scrum toward the wine? Yes. Yes, it was awkward. It was funny. We were at a last-minute party for a SCAD grad held in lieu of a ceremony and a bigger party. It was, for me, the last gathering of any sort. We tried to be careful. We pretended to be careful. But at the time, it all seemed so ridiculous and overplayed.

Now we are spraying—or wondering if we should be spraying—the packaging of our food. There seems to be a variety of opinions on that one. Now we are talking to people on the phone—a lost activity—or texting before we call to see if it's a good time (this when we have lots of time) to call. Now we are dropping notes—a postcard here, a postcard there—the kind of missives that need stamps—to check on people. Some of us are starting to avoid walks around the park. Too many people. Instead we venture into nearby neighborhoods we don't really know about. We are continuing our discussion about the potency of a droplet. Since our Georgia governor—not a fan of science—made the news, we are hearing from long-lost friends asking sarcastically if we're heading out for a manicure, a round of bowling or, perhaps, a tattoo, maybe with the number 19 for this iteration of the COVID virus.

Last week, for fun—and variety—three of us met spontaneously for cocktails in a downtown square. Our "host"—the person who lives on the square—had to provide the libations. Without much protest, Gary provided martinis in a lovely lustreware pitcher resting on a silver tray, along with some home-roasted peanuts. Some late-blooming azaleas were putting on a show in competition with the trees overhead. There's so much more to see in the squares when you are the only people there. I'm not sure any of us has ever gathered at cocktail hour before in such a grand setting. No gnats either. Very civilized, very continental. We like to think of our squares as places of conviviality, but most of the time they're too crowded—with people from out of town (nothing wrong with that, mind you) looking at maps, at phones, at historical markers—to enjoy them ourselves. It was very, very quiet. Hey, are we taking back the town? Wouldn't that be a kick: people moving back downtown into their rental or Airbnb properties? While it's not a great time to publish a new book or release a new movie, we do have time to indulge in both. But after nearly a month of both platforms, I have to ask: Why are there still so many books and movies centering around the Nazis? Or does it just seem that way? HBO's six-part series *The Plot Against America* is based on Philip Roth's novel from 2004. In the book Charles Lindbergh, a hero for his non-stop solo flight across the Atlantic Ocean, has won the presidency on an isolationist ticket (Lindbergh's base was known as America First; sound familiar?) that targeted Jews, Blacks and immigrants. Walter Winchell, a well-known radio broadcaster at the time (and Jewish), who was running against him, was killed. Lots of grueling Ku Klux Klan scenes.

Then there's *Resistance*. It's about Marcel Marceau, a French mime (also Jewish) who helped lead hundreds of Jewish children over the mountains into Switzerland. And *JoJo Rabbit*, a satiric treatment about a Hitler Youth member who finds out his mother is hiding a Jewish girl in the family home.

Three wouldn't have been so bad except the book club I'm in just finished reading *The Nightingale*, also set in the late '30s, also in Vichy France, about two sisters. One stays in her small town, the other leads hundreds of orphaned children to safety.

Just when I was thinking it might be time for a little Jane Austen, a friend in Durham raved about *The Seventh Cross* by Anna Seghers, a German author, published in 1942, about—you guessed it—Nazi Germany in 1936. He'll send it when he finishes.

5/2/20

8 / *If only I'd asked about the Purple Gang (These are the over-thinking days)*

With nothing but time on our hands, these pandemic days have become the "if only" days. There are just so many drawers to straighten, shelves to organize, onion pies to bake before ennui sets in. If only I had bought the house next door for more gardening space. If only I could read my handwriting in a myriad of small notebooks. If only I had organized my photographs better.

If only I had asked my grandparents more questions. Oh, I tried. All I got was, "When the Russians wanted me to fight in its army after hunting us down in the pogroms, I left home," my grandfather would say. He was 16. Maybe it was 1907.

Then what? I asked.

"I walked to London," he answered.

You walked to London, I repeated. From Poland (or maybe Russia, which is what his naturalization papers said). Across Europe. Across the English Channel. Then what?

London made him sneeze, he said. It was bad for his allergies. "I knew someone in Detroit, so I went there through Montreal."
That's it. That's all I know.

At 18 he couldn't read or write English. He started peddling junk. He started a steel company. When he saved some money, he brought his brother Saul (or maybe it was Solomon) over from the "old country." There were a lot of men in our family named Saul, so we called him Sam, except sometimes it was Saul-from-Windsor. They looked alike, both short. Every year Saul-from-Windsor's daughters kissed the ground and thanked my grandfather for bringing them to this country.

That's it. That's what I know. He wasn't someone who wanted to "nurse and rehearse." Yiddish? Forget about it. Speak English. That was then, this is now.

If only I had pinned him down. It's not as if we didn't spend time with him or my grandmother. We lived blocks away. They came over for dinner every Friday night. My mother and grandmother seemed to talk every day (sometimes I listened on the upstairs landline). They played bridge. They went shopping at Hudson's. They went to the Fisher Building. We joked about my grandfather talking to his "book- ie" with his hand cupped over the phone so we wouldn't hear—or maybe it was his stock broker. He went to the shvitz, the steam bath, also at the Fisher Building. Now people call the shvitz— still in exis- tence—an urban health club. It opened in 1930, which would have been about right. It was home, I read, to the Purple Gang, a Jewish mob known for bootlegging and hijacking.

My grandfather never mentioned the Purple Gang.

If only I had asked him about the Purple Gang. If only I had asked my grandmother more about her history. She was also mum, but she made good chopped liver.

If only I had asked my mother more. When I read people's mem- ories during Mother's Day, I'm jealous. I wonder why I don't have more memories of my own. We weren't estranged, just maybe a little defensive and uncertain. Both of us. She was generous with money when I needed it, though I rarely asked. I guess I just wanted to figure things out for myself; I knew early on her way wasn't my way. I have photographs, black-and-white portrait shots of her with rouged cheeks and slinky dresses. I remember her sisters, Joan and Mildred, and her brothers, Saul (another Saul) and Harry. I know she liked to travel to Europe with her friends, that they booked the trips through Bee Kalt Travel Agency. (I still have the monogrammed travel bag), that she was a good bridge player, that she subscribed to The New Yorker ("Do you understand the jokes?" she once wrote to me. "I don't."), that she used a three-ring notebook to keep track of her stocks.

I know her handwriting as well as I know my own. We wrote

letters. I still have her recipe for banana bread written on the back of one of my sister's high school graduation photographs, so thrifty was she. She visited me everywhere I lived. Every time I make a U-turn, I remember her saying, "Can you do that in Savannah? We can't."

I have her shell collection, a lamp, an ashtray, her brooches, her swimming goggles and six pairs of glasses (including a pair of sunglasses that folds up) spanning the decades and styles. When I see those glasses, I see her clear as day.

She wasn't the type—neither was I—to end a phone conversation with "I love you" and that's fine. I don't regret that. If only I had known her a little better. If only I had asked more questions.

5/17/20

9 / *Covid and dog days*
duke it out
(Grasping at straws, anything)

Fatigue is setting in. A few months ago, I was looking for joy. Now I realize I might have been setting my sights too high. Now I'll settle for a drive to Ellabell, Georgia, just to look at those clouds, even if it's the same clouds I see at home, even if it means I'm passing burnt, midsummer fields and, worse yet, piles of trees, indiscriminately sheared down, lying helter-skelter, higgledy-piggledy. The reason those trees have to come down? Safety, the state Department of Transportation says, so when there's an accident drivers don't veer into them and hurt themselves. Huh? That is what you call a cockamamie explanation. You may as well never drive a car because you might have an accident; that would solve the problem. Goodbye, noise buffers. Goodbye, shade. Goodbye, beautiful natural air filtration and water runoff solution.

Why don't we just cut down all the trees and make I-16 a veritable speedway? Could we maybe think about a campaign to enforce the speed limit?

Next plan. This week I made a visit to Brighter Day Natural Foods Market to buy some groceries IN PERSON. Shopping was never more fun. My cousin on St. Simons Island said he counts his weekly trip to Harris Teeter as his vacation. For me, nothing beats the Tuesday stop at Vertu Farm, an old-fashioned vegetable stand—they also offer sausage from Whippoorwill Farms and meat from Savannah River Farms—with pleasant, young farmers who could complain but don't. It sits in a beautiful spot off one of those confounded state streets (where I frequently get lost) along Bonaventure Road. This morning I wrote the streets on my hand. So now I know. Turn east on Georgia Avenue, then right on Tennessee Avenue. It's where the For-syth Farmers' Market has—or used to have—its fundraising picnic. There's never more than two or three people at a time. Same with the Wednesday Farm Truck 912 on Bee Road. Vertu Farm also has the occasional popup market on Friday night.

To make things more challenging, we've entered the dog days, that celestial period from the middle of July through early September. Can you say lethargy, mad dogs, bad luck? Dog days, meet the pan-demic. Nice to share this month with you, dog days. Let's see who can wreak the most havoc.

The world will never be the same, sings Lin-Manuel Miranda in *Hamilton*, his improbable hit musical about the complex Alexander Hamilton—an immigrant, by the way. But here's some good news: We can watch the Broadway production for free on the Disney+ channel. Free, if you join. Yep. All you need to do is subscribe for one month at $6.99, then you can drop out. Since the world has gone platform cra-zy, if you want to pay $7 more you can get Hulu and ESPN. Always a gimmick. Well worth $6.99. I've watched it twice so far. Even if you can't follow the rapid-fire rapping dialogue, it's worth it for the chore-ography, the costumes, the voices, the energy, the originality, the light-ing, the history, such as it is. Subtitles help.

"Things change," sings Miranda. True. I won't always be getting "shelter in place" checks from my insurance company. Checks like $14.12 and $13.67. Woo-hoo. I won't always be going to a drive-thru bank because maybe someday my downtown branch will open and I can look a teller in the eyes again. I won't always be wondering: Will we/I be around to see how everything turns out? Would that our days were like a movie we were watching at home, one where we could stop and check how much longer it ran and, if we wished, to see how it ended.

Was it just a few months ago we thought we might be able to sit far enough apart for a Passover seder? A book club session? A dinner party? We do seem to be talking to one another on the phone more often than texting. That's a good thing. And the talking we're doing when walking or sitting on the front porch seems more consequential and serious than the normal in-person group socializing, which in more normal times takes up a lot of our day.

Now the simplest things make me happy: hearing the music on television nature shows when I'm in the other room; stopping for a traffic light with my window open and hearing someone in the next car over say, "Hey, Miss Jane. Miss you."

But just between us chickens, I don't think I'll ever get used to wearing a mask, even though I do wear one and have multiple choices to "go with my outfit." It's a good time to get a tooth pulled or hide a pimple. Dog days. COVID. Both of you: get thee behind me. Soon.

7/26/20

10 / *More COVID craziness (shit's getting real)*

I don't know about you but I'd give my upper left molar (if I had one) to claim a Jamaican father, an Indian mother, a Jewish mother-in-law I like to cook with, and two stepchildren named after Ella Fitzgerald and John Coltrane (Ella and Cole) who call me Momala, as in Kamala Harris, one of our choices for vice president. It's the American story.

Welcome to 2020, where the whole fricking world is farmisht, Yiddish for "cockeyed," "messed-up," "crazy," where the term "good trouble" (thank you, John Lewis) is a good thing, something we need more of, not less. And that's on a good day.

Where the most popular restaurant I see from the road—are you ready for this, all you foodies?—is Popeyes. I should only be so lucky not to get into an accident with all the cars wrapped around that red-and-yellow building on Victory Drive, a line so long it almost extends into Wendy's, the restaurant next door. The 47-year-old New Orleans chain, now owned by America's Favorite Chicken Company, has struck a nerve. They even sell crawfish, or so I read somewhere.

The pandemic of 2020: where the double bill at the Jesup drive-in theater ("Georgia's oldest," circa 1949) is "Beauty and the Beast" and "Bohemian Rhapsody," with popcorn, pizza, nachos, burgers and all the fried food you could want at the ready. Too bad the August summer sun hangs so long in the sky. Can't show the movie on the outdoor screen until dark descends. The first feature doesn't begin until 8:45, the second at 11:08. Too late for me. We lose one minute of sunlight a day. Pretty soon it will be within my range.

Welcome to the tail end of the dog days: where the most reliable plant this month—except for zinnias—is the undemanding native poinsettia. No water required. No fertilizer. No sun. No shade. She pops up every year around this time to add a little color to our lives and to remind us the real poinsettia season—which means colder temps, aka winter—is just a few months away.

This is the month I get an official "Important tax return document" from my bank announcing 2019 earnings on an IRA contribution of $10.09. I know we had an extension for filing our income tax returns this year, but I'm not sure that's what they were thinking when they got around to sending this. I'm getting this now? In August?

This is when there's a run on elderberry, the new "it" herb for COVID. The berries, so I read, are good for boosting your immune system, lessening stress, protecting your heart. If you can find any.

When the most fun I've had in months is venturing out to an indoor market where I stand in front of an aisle of food—so many types of apples, so many potatoes, so many varieties of pasta—uncertain of how to act in public, how to choose. After ordering food online for so many months, I get to make my own choices. On one of those online orders, I checked "honey" and "yogurt" but what I got were one of those little honey bears and a carton of honey yogurt (which turned out to be a hit).

This is COVID craziness: where it's hard to buy a bike, used or new, because the supply chain—that phrase we learned back in March, remember?—mainly from China, has been interrupted, hindered, messed with. Don't get me wrong: It's a good thing we're riding bikes. But this is America, where we've been brought up to think we can buy anything we want anytime.

Where staying at home means the best place to see a really good sunset, if you live in the city, is looking west down your east-west lane. Where the clouds are lush and lavish and the ocean is at a most delicious temperature (just on the verge of being too warm)—except now we have to look out for the trailing tentacles of a jellyfish. Ouch! Get your white vinegar ready. Get ready to make a paste with the wet sand and bury yourself mermaid-style to mitigate the sting (much more fun than smearing on tobacco juice or baking soda). Surely someone somewhere is eating—not cursing—those jellyfish. Or has that supply chain been disrupted, too?

8/23/20

"Cent anni, al meno.
A hundred years, at least.

PASSAGES

1 / *Be here now and things change: Lois Hauselman*

When a cousin of mine asked for some words of advice to put in a book for her dear mother, who is turning 70, all I could think of was my old standby: Be here now and things change. Both reference the time my partner Billy and I ran a restaurant in Eureka Springs, Arkansas, the Pita Hut. When business was good and we were so busy we couldn't think straight, we had to focus on the moment, to prep for the next day, to go to the store to pick up more onions, carrots or bananas. When business was not so good and we worried if we could pay our bills or if we even wanted to continue, we'd say, "Well, tomorrow's another day, things will change."

Right about the time I offered these modest words of wisdom for cousin Nancy, I read an article from someone who is living with cancer, something writer Christopher Hitchens called a "double frame" of mind—surviving in the present and preparing for death. It seemed apt.

African Americans may know this as "double consciousness." This is a term W.E.B. Du Bois coined to explain how it feels to live in a racist society. Toni Morrison talked about not worrying about the "white gaze," preferring to write for other African Americans.

All the rest of us know is this: We're going to die. Sometime. So we might as well live—even with the hovering threat of bad news, personally and universally. For me, this summer seems to be rife with bad news. Two friends diagnosed with early-onset dementia, another with giardia, a third in a full-leg cast from a botched knee replacement operation, a fourth recovering from shoulder surgery.

What's going on? I text someone who had just told me about friends who were hospitalized with blood clots, uterine fibroids and a bum hip.

Maybe because we're older? I say. Or we know more people so the odds are good we'll know more people who are ill?

Or, she answered, the availability of more procedures?

Before this summer, I might have offered my cousin a third observation: Bad news travels fast. That's before I found out about Lois. I had met Lois at a tennis tournament in Chicago's Waveland Park. We were opponents. She had a crazy windup service motion. I forget who won. But she—a bit older, a writer, an artist, married, long settled in Chicago—generously took me (a newcomer to the city, with few friends or contacts) into her life. We started a softball team we called "the over-the-hill team." We met Wednesday nights to play indoor tennis on Fullerton Avenue. We talked about books, writing, life. In 1973, we watched on television as Billie Jean King trounced Bobby Riggs in straight sets.

We became tennis partners on one team or another. During her eighth month of pregnancy with Nicholas, her third child, we won some local tournament. We laughed thinking we might have freaked out our opponents if they had known about her pending birth.

I left Chicago before I got to know any of her children. When I returned to town, I'd pop over spontaneously for the occasional visit. In between, we'd write long catch-up letters on multiple pieces of lined paper with lots of arrows and inserted words. I had trouble reading some of it because neither of us had the best penmanship. Her life was full. She became president of a northside synagogue. Her children had children. She and her husband took bike trips around the world.

I didn't think that much about her. And then sometime in the middle of the night when I couldn't sleep, I Googled her. Just to get a little Lois magic, some good Lois juju. That's when I saw the headline OBITUARY. I was sure it was a mistake. It couldn't be. This couldn't be the Lois I knew. I read through the comments on the funeral home's website for confirmation, desperate to know how she died. I needed more. No one was saying. I called a friend in common. Cancer.

In our brief time together, we talked about a lot of things. We shared certain (not all) secrets. We cried, searching for words to match feelings. We did not bring up death. Why would we? We thought we would live forever. I've lost other friends, but this is a hard one. I thought I was OK until I stayed with someone who had an old wooden tennis racket in the house, a Billie Jean King model we both used. I missed her all over again.

That's when I decided I'm going to ignore the headline "OBIT-UARY." Since she had flown this earth for months before I read the news, I decided I'm going to live in that "double frame" of mind. I going to adopt Du Bois' "double consciousness." I'm going to carry on as if she were still here, because in some way she still is. And like many people we love who cross over, she always will be.

8/18/19

A HAIKU FOR DAVID

happy birthday, starnes
oh, to see your face again
got any cookies?

2 / David Starnes

In the end, it's not about property, not about title, not about net worth or resources. It's not about who you know. Though maybe I'm wrong about that last part, because a few days ago when someone behind me at Gamble Funeral Service, her blue eyes spilling over, leaned forward and whispered, "I didn't know you knew David," she might well have been channeling many people's thoughts.

Because that's how David Starnes lived his life. Private. Singular. Mysterious. He didn't advertise what or who he knew. He wasn't one to tell stories out of school. He was too smart for that. He knew that things change but friendships are forever. He knew that words carry weight, that once uttered, words are tucked away and remembered.

He could see the big picture. Yet he knew the value of the personal, the details. If you didn't see him for months or years, if you weren't privy to the occasional "Starnes sighting," as we were wont to say, so rare was he in town the last few years after he started teaching English at Georgia Southern University, so lucky did we feel if we caught a glimpse of that loping, loopy, slightly offbeat, low-to-the-ground walk, those dancing eyebrows and ironic eyes, the easy, well-timed pratfall, then surely you could count on a birthday card—even, I understand, an anniversary card. Every year. (How many people send anniversary cards?).

This, no matter how many times your address, your city, your zip code changed, no matter how many times you forgot to send him a card on his birthday.

When I heard about his death in a car accident some two weeks after my birthday—which falls one day before his—I knew I would return home from an extended out-of-town trip to find a birthday card, and I did. It was stamped with Judy Garland, penned in his familiar script, addressed on the inside, as always, to Jane F., signed as usual, "Love, David S."

"Where are you," he said, "and what did you learn today and how come you don't write?"

This year's Christmas card from David, filled with words circling around themselves, seemed to imbue a greater-than-usual sense of hope. It was a Xeroxed copy of the classic Annie Leibovitz photo of John and Yoko spooning and the words, never more appropriate, "Give peace a chance."

This past week of mourning and celebrating, I heard talk of a lot of David details. On the day of his funeral, one special friend of his allowed, quietly, "Everything I'm wearing David gave to me." Bracelet, pendant, earrings, skirt, blouse. And love.

As it turns out, the man we always regarded as shy and private was anything but a recluse. He was as apt to show up in my garden for a chat under the shade of the spreading sycamore tree as he was to appear at another friend's front door asking his trademark question, "Got any cookies?" There were other visits in the garden near Charlie's former wooden kayak factory, like the time when we each reached behind the front seat of our individual cars found our baseball mitts and played catch.

But because David Starnes, who had just turned 64 at the time of his death, was complicated and always changing, always growing, I never knew the effect nor imagined the consequences he could have on young, first-time writers or not-so-young first-time writers.

To echo the words of Cormac McCarthy in *The Road*: Starnes was one of the good people, carrying the flame of hope and life in a world that sometimes appears filled with despair and despondency.

I met him during one of his many transitional periods when, in between writing poems and contemplating a return to school, he was doing carpentry and painting houses. I met him when he and friend Charlie Reeves gave a client of theirs (a client with a good sense of humor) a box of calling cards advertising their services. Their motto?

"We're slow but we're expensive."

But what I heard from students at the funeral, as pitch-perfect a celebration as any I've been to, signaled a different David Starnes, one who could inspire and influence, applaud and appreciate. A mentor. Because he did not own property, Starnes had time to canoe, to kayak, to write poetry. Because he did not have kids, he could consider renting a Santa Claus suit, which he did, pop up at friends' homes and, unbidden, unexpected, unasked, do his thing.

"He is the freest man I know," said his father.

Because he was not married, he could spend more time with more friends, which he was doing the last night of his life.

"This is as good as it gets," someone who was at that dinner recalled him saying.

During the funeral, Kristina Beaty sang a haunting and prophetic version of Irving Berlin's song, "What'll I Do?" and it was lovely. I sort of wish we could have also heard the Beatles' "When I'm Sixty-Four," which is what I find myself humming today.

I know I'm not the only one singing it to you, Starnes.

5/23/07

A PRICK AND A DIBBLE

"The answer to one of my biggest dilemmas—how to transplant seedlings before their roots wrap around each other and while they still have a chance to grow big and strong. "Pricking" is a garden term I just learned from George Wilson. It means sticking something pointed like a letter opener into the pot of seedlings and separating an individual plant. Then you pick up your wooden dibble—great word—and with the blunt end make a depression in a larger pot, which is where your new fledgling seedling is planted. All of this standing up, not lying flat on the ground, separating the twisted seedlings. But really: prick? Reminds me of a political sign I saw in Pittsburgh for the feckless Rick Perry. It read, "Dump Rick." But if you read it fast, well, try it. It comes out, "Dumb Prick."

3 / George Wilson

At this point in my life I've known quite a few people who have passed on. Sometimes during a long road trip in the car when I'm by myself, I'll count on my fingers how many. Then, because it takes more than two hands, I'll lose track. My mind drifts. I move on before circling back to asking, "What's the point?" Except for the chance to remember them, which is nice, precisely the reason behind the Jewish tradition of leaving a stone on a tombstone when visiting folks in the cemetery, to show someone remembered them.

Some of those people died suddenly. No chance for a visit, a recap. Others lived out of town. No way to visit them, either. Still others, in the throes of sickness, hospitals, IV tubes, confusion, pain, various levels of consciousness, were beyond visiting.

Which makes my last visit with George Wilson—friend, gardener, baker, philosopher, contrarian, traveler, iconoclast—all the more special. When I heard he was receiving hospice care, I didn't give myself a chance to think what that meant or what shape he might be in. I didn't want to overthink the situation. I picked up the phone and called him. He answered.

"How about a visit?" I said.

"When?" he asked.

"Now," I said. "Fifteen minutes?"

As much as anyone, George exemplified the personal aspect of the Saturday Forsyth Farmers' Market. He didn't come as a commercial farmer with acres and acres of land to tend; he grew vegetables in his backyard, a brilliant example of all that someone can produce in a small space. He didn't arrive with tons of greens. Yes, he had collards and kale and okra, but he also had frisée (or curly endive), escarole, tatsoi and edible flowers like borage blooms, pansies, nasturtiums and yellow squash blossoms. He wasn't supporting a family on this income; he was there for the relationships he developed. His customers loved him; he loved them. He missed them when he was out of town or when he didn't have enough to bring to market.

I didn't know what to expect when I knocked on his door. George and his husband Jake live "on the other side" of Martin Luther King, Jr. Blvd., the west side, which bespeaks a certain racial divide that he never considered. He wanted a big house when he moved here from Atlanta, he told me, "so we could have roommates, community." And that rambling Victorian house did it. That word again, community. For years they rented (and befriended) travelers from all over the world. "Why would we want to just be here by ourselves?" he'd say. "That's no fun."

A few months before our last visit, I went over to weed around the hibiscus or sorrel shrub we both love so much. A few weeks later, I returned and watched him put in some veggies he had started inside by seed. I watched him hoe a row, slowly, then scatter some dry granular fertilizer before setting the plants down, so much more careful and deliberate than I. He was planting in an old swimming pool he and Jake filled up with horse manure and other composted material.

He looked thin when he answered the door, but he seemed happy to see me. We plopped down in two comfy chairs. He took my hands and we sat, knees to knees. The last time I saw him, at the market, he said he had a turkey for our annual Chanukah party, which we didn't have this year. To go to one of his birthday parties—where he cooked—was a treat. He would make beef bourguignon, coq au vin, venison chili. He even made his own birthday cake, Julia Child's orange Bavarian cream. He loved telling the story about the time Julia Child was supposed to come to the French restaurant he owned in Atlanta. He prepped and cooked all day only to learn she had to cancel.

For the next hour—maybe 90 minutes—we talked. He was in good spirits, openly relieved hospice had arrived, effusively complimentary of their work, happy for Jake to have assistance. We talked of parents, friends, gardens, Qigong. He said how tired he was. He said I could have some of his ashes for my gardens. He was looking forward to rice and beans for dinner with some leftover chicken. He already knew who he wanted at his funeral. "Yeah," I said. "Everyone but you!"

He sent me home with some gerbera daisies.

Two days later, after he passed, I returned to the house to see Jake, who had sung "Plant a Radish" from *The Fantasticks* at his funeral. We hugged, cried, relived George's last night. Before I left, we headed to the little greenhouse room off the kitchen. Jake wanted to send me home with some of George's seedlings, a flat of mizuna. They're already in the ground.

2/16/20

4 / Joan Cobitz

Joan Cobitz, a first-rate storyteller who never took a shortcut in her narratives, gifted baker, in-house psychoanalyst, resident coffeehouse pundit and true connoisseur of pithy one-liners, died Monday morning not five weeks after holding forth in the hospital as if it were a salon, surrounded by friends bearing bags of take-out Thai food, vessels of homemade chicken soup and bowls of steaming rice with freshly picked broccoli. She was being treated for cancer.

People gravitated toward Joan for advice (sought or not); for her strangely perverse good humor; for a contrary and unpredictable point of view. She was thoughtful. While dunking a biscotti in coffee, sitting with her dog Sage (or Mango or Chutney) and looking for just the right word, she'd tilt her head back, fix her eyes skyward and preface her observations with, "I want to say..." Which she would follow up with, "You remember the joke..." For people with whom she had no sympathy, Joan, 72, delivered two words: "Poor beast." The bread she produced every Wednesday and Friday afternoon at Brighter Day Natural Foods Market was legendary. Knowing there were limited loaves, devotees would start meandering into the store early in the day, hoping to catch it just right. Everyone had a favorite. Italian cornbread. Raisin-walnut. Seven-grain flax. Sourdough French. The occasional cinnamon roll. If a child appeared curious—or restless—in the store, Joan, who also baked for The DeSoto hotel, would hand over a hunk of dough to knead. She was generous with her recipes, too, anxious to pass along what she knew. "She was pleased to replace herself," said her sister, Gail Pickus.

During her hospital stay, Joan reminded the folks at Brighter Day to post the sign, "Joan will not be baking bread today."

"She essentially raised me," said Gail, 16 months younger. "If something was playing on the radio that she'd told me about, she'd turn to me and say sharply, 'What is that!?' We'd go toe-to-toe occasionally, but then she'd spit back, 'Listen, missy, don't mimic me.'" This past Tuesday, instead of her cache of wax-paper-wrapped loaves huddling on her baking tray, there was a bouquet of forsythia and spirea. Her signature desserts included a strawberry charlotte, lemon bombe, orange Marsala cake, flourless chocolate cake, Stollen and a Linzer torte, which she'd occasionally FedEx to her son, Tony, in a specially rigged cardboard box, especially when he was trying to impress a new girlfriend.

For her Thursday night supper club, Joan would bring clam spaghetti, bouillabaisse, white bean and kale soup, baked and stuffed mackerel, lamb stew, and seasonal chutneys and preserves. She was a fearless cook, not unlike her grandmother, Ethel Hamilton, who emigrated from Odessa, Ukraine, settling first in Gary, Indiana—where, with no money, she opened a deli—then Chicago, where Joan was raised. Like her father Boris, an advertising artist who would paint dishes like coq au vin on the linoleum floors of their rented apartment, Joan had an active mind and a gift for art. She studied with Mauricio Lasansky at the University of Iowa, where she earned a master's degree in printmaking. She was one of the early instructors at the then-fledgling Savannah College of Art and Design. Several years ago, she curated a major show at the Telfair Museum on the work of the celebrated and late artist Larry Connatser, Joan's companion for 35 years.

She was uncompromising in her baking and her opinions, and if she wasn't the first to say, "Yadda, yadda, yadda," she might as well have been. She rarely gave an offhand compliment. "She could be blunt and still not hurt someone's feelings," said Janie Brodhead, co-owner of Brighter Day. "I learned from Joan that everyone doesn't have to be so nice all the time. She taught us a lot."

4/11/05

5 / Jim Bitler

One Sunday afternoon, no different than any other, Jim Bitler, the face of Ossabaw Island, the on-island working stiff of the Ossabaw Island Foundation who wore Crocs and shorts in all kinds of weather and never seemed to get any mosquito or chigger bites, the go-to man for Eleanor Sandy West (who gifted the island to the state of Georgia in 1978), died while taking a nap. He was 55. Paul Pressly, the Foundation's Education Alliance Director, was on the island at the time. Pressly knew something was amiss after he called Bitler repeatedly, only to get Jim's upbeat and unmistakable message: "If I don't answer, chances are I am somewhere on this beautiful island loving my job."

Few can boast so much love for what they do. Accompanied by his two Boston terriers, Beau ("that's Beau-regardless," he would say) and Kate ("Katherine the Great"), Bitler would greet visitors at the dock, standing there, waving them in. He'd load them in his truck, drive them to their quarters and start the magic. Through him, the island's history came alive. He was scientist, raconteur and naturalist. He could point out the island's eleven longleaf pine trees. He knew the gestation period of an armadillo (up to one hundred and twenty days), how to identify and cook "chicken of the tree" (an island mushroom) and just the right amount of oyster shells, lime, sand and water to recreate the original tabby surface of the three standing slave cabins on the island's north end. Once he caught a baby piglet by the side of the road and held it up for all to see before letting it go. He taught himself to weave sweet grass baskets and knew where the sweet grass grew.

His quarters were simple, his mind a steel-trap retrieval system. He was a stand-up comedian. If he bumped up a story a notch or two, it was only to make it better. No one seemed to mind.

To Mrs. West, his longtime compatriot and co-conspirator, the impish Bitler was "Pieface" or "James James Morrison Morrison Wetherby George Dupree" from A.A. Milne. He was a watercolorist. He discovered a particular strain of indigo that had been growing under everyone's noses, then published it in the New Georgia Encyclopedia. Bitler, who spent seven years at Ossabaw, graduated from Ohio State University with a degree in something related to wilderness skills. As a naturalist, he worked on Little St. Simons Island, and for Wilderness Southeast, the Sea Island Company and Disney's Hilton Head Resort. That, he liked to say, is where he was employee of the year, "which meant I had to walk across the stage in giant Mickey Mouse shoes in front of Maya Angelou, who was speaking." If he never said it, he lived it: be here now, love what you do.

4/12/11

6 / Judy Mooney

In the end, it was her grip. It was strong. It was firm. She wasn't letting go. Until the last day of her life Judy Mooney, who passed away two weeks ago, never wanted to lose that connection. It felt like a direct line to her soul. If she didn't have the strength to talk, she wanted to touch. But that makes sense. This woman was a sculptor. She could shape a nose that looks like a nose. She could catch an expression—pain, fatigue, determination, angst. She could create a gesture. She had a feel for figures from the Gullah culture. She didn't shy away from complexity or challenge. Witness the piece she called "Rosa Parks, Back of the Bus," multiple figures, each small, each detailed.

She could shape a mean and tasty crab cake, too, even if she didn't eat them.

To look at the bronze and ceramic figures in her Ardsley Park living room, you'd think she had been doing this her whole life. Wrong. She went from the corporate world to the artist studio, from dressing for success as the Vice President of Community Development at the YMCA in Charlotte, to sitting behind a potter's wheel with a glazing tong, a wooden knife, a sponge, all within arm's length. She moved from overseeing budgets and supervising staff to organizing artist workshops at Wildacres Retreat in North Carolina, dealing with area galleries that still have her work, and holing up in her studio.

Did she have any idea this is what she would do, that this would become her passion? I asked this question, again and again. It's a real issue for people who jump off the treadwheel, who find themselves with time, who have to invent the day. Nope, she said. She just wanted to take some art classes. So she did—at Armstrong State University, now part of Georgia Southern University. Her world—and that of her husband, Pat, an able companion—turned to art. With matching ponytails, Birkenstocks and one car between them (Pat rode his bike to work), they could be seen at most openings. They were a team.

When she started undergoing treatment for cancer, she cut her hair to anticipate a loss of hair that never happened. Pat cut his, too. He supported her treatment; she indulged his humor.

Pat is a jokester, a jester, a listener. For years he worked as a mental health counselor at SCAD, but Pat took it a step further. During exams, he morphed into the Pizza Fairy, delivering boxes of pizza to the library, the dorm, the student center. He had his stock jokes. He could wiggle his ears, sing wacky birthday songs, tell a story at the drop of a hat. Judy would roll her eyes, roll with Pat.

He could ride his bike forever. When they met thirty-five years ago in Louisiana, neither was interested in marrying a second time. They worked on charity rides, triathlons, fundraisers. They started training together. They started taking individually mapped weeklong bike rides all over the country with friends.

To Judy, he was "Pat Mooney," two names, first and last.

To her grandchildren, she was Meems, and Pat was Bebop because he used to sing the kids to sleep but not before a tickle and a belly laugh.

When the couple moved to Savannah, they might have had twelve bikes between them: mountain bikes, tandems, racing bikes.

They continued to pedal. When Judy was about to turn 70, she decided to ride in the annual seventy-mile bike ride in and around Savannah. She recruited me and others. We trained—sort of—on Sundays, riding around the base at Hunter Army Airfield, stopping for coffee at Starbucks at Twelve Oaks Shopping Center, giving one another pep talks.

And then the cancer hit. They threw everything they had at it. In between procedures, Pat stuck around the house, played his guitar, supervised her supplements, quit his job ("We don't know how long Judy will have. I want to be here"). Judy talked about getting back into the studio. People visited. Children, grandchildren, artist friends. Again and again. She made it to her seventy-sixth birthday, in July, when no one thought she would, then to Pat's sixty-ninth, then to their anniversary: thirty-two years. She went from avocados to ice cream to chips of ice. As she lost weight, her blue eyes got bigger and brighter. She could still whisper, "I love you." When someone mentioned a mutual friend's intention to visit, she mouthed the words, "Tell her not to wait too long."

In the last few days, her grip started to give way. She was growing weak. The connection was lessening. She could no longer hold on.

When Pat's phone call came—"Judy has gone on to that giant sculptor's studio in the sky"—I was not surprised. But I was and am sad. I still think about dropping by that living room. I still want to hold that hand.

8/27/17

7 / *Ronnie Kronowitz*

It's popular, I know, to read the obituaries in the newspaper, to keep up. Just not my style. I'm more of the "bad news travels fast" kind of gal. I know a goodly number of people who are ill or struggling. And I keep up with them. Sort of. The best I can. But how do you stay in touch with the people who are not in poor health, who are not below par, not on anyone's sick list, who are not going anywhere but forward? Why would I waste time worrying about them? Those are the people you expect to be with us forever. Wrong, I know. But it's a fact.

That's what we think. People who explore, change course in their 70s, rent an apartment in New York City, go to the opera in Santa Fe, sell properties and then buy more in Budapest. Budapest! Of all places.

Ronnie Kronowitz, you were not supposed to die. You are supposed to be here to listen to my complaints, to laugh at my jokes, to commiserate with me about the world's fakakta ways. It's not that we were close friends but we liked one another, especially when I learned you were born in Chicago, which meant we shared a few Midwestern traits. But that's the way it is in Savannah. There are people you see sporadically, but when you do see them you can pick up the same conversation you had a year ago. Two years ago. These are people who can finish your sentence.

You could finish my sentences. You were leading the way for the rest of us, showing us how to regroup, refocus, rekindle. You of the many opinions, the broad gestures, the eager ear, the good taste in art; you, the traveler. You could show up in Savannah out of the blue (to me, at least, not to your family or good friends or neighbors on Bull

Street), walk around Forsyth Park, go to a concert, visit your son Lowell's store on Broughton Street, shake your finger at me and say none too quietly, "What's going on?" (and mean it) or "Why haven't you visited me in Budapest?" (and really want to know that, too). I dutifully transferred all your information into my phone's contact list, and you added me to your legion of "friends" on Facebook. ("Aren't we modern?" you said)

The last time I saw you, we were at some gathering—there is no dearth of gatherings in this little/big town—and you said, "Who are these people? I don't even know them." That's when I said, "Isn't that great? That you or I don't know them?" and you shook your head because you knew what I meant. We like our circles. We like our clan. Because we've been here a while, we think we know Savannah. But it's changing. New people are popping up and popping out all the time and it's exciting. Still, we have to note it because we remember when it wasn't quite so exciting.

I have no memory of how we met, how we started talking. I'm not from here, not in your work circle, not in your family (maybe your tribe but not your family). I didn't go to your synagogue. I did live across the street from you and Bailee, your wife, on Jones Street when I first moved to town. That's when you lived next to Gloria and Ben Tucker. I would see Bailee during the day. I went to some of her cooking classes at your house. But I didn't see you. I think you were in your heavy work phase back then. You weren't on the street much.

Except Forsyth Park. You were a regular there. And you would kibitz. You would say, "How's your mother? I want to know more about your mother," because that's when I was writing about my Jewish mother (who passed away in 2010) and everyone can relate to the Jewish mother thing. When Lowell moved to town, you would say, "You've got another University of Michigan compatriot. Are you watching the game? It's on today."

I don't like that you're not here, Ronnie. I know. Me, me, me, right? If you were here, I would tell you how I teared up when your grandchildren—also teary—talked about you, their Papa, especially when your granddaughter said you told her, "Don't pay any attention to what people think." I would say how many people turned up at Bonaventure Cemetery for your funeral. I would say, "What are we going to do the next four years?" and, "Maybe it's time to buy stock in blood pressure medicine."

But Lowell got us off the hook. He said—and I thought it was pitch-perfect—that he didn't want anyone crying to him about you. Instead, he wanted to hear Ronnie stories. I know there are plenty of them out there. Still, I'd rather be telling them to you.

2/4/17

8 / Boo Hornstein

You were a happier person if you ran into Boo Hornstein on the street. He had a common touch, a good story, a sly, understated grin that said, "Hey, life's not so bad, eh?" He was a sweet man with gentle eyes, a keen wit. He was funny but not snarky funny, not funny at the expense of anyone else. He didn't overexplain. He didn't say things to win points or knock you over with his knowledge, although he knew a lot, especially about Savannah's old City Market, jazz and baseball, especially about Savannah. As a lifelong resident of Gaston Street, living in the same house his whole life, he could have set the story straight many times about the way things used to be in the city. But he didn't. Not his style.

He had the outward credentials of a highly polished professional social worker—the doctorate, the university professor jobs, the titles, the awards, the recognitions—but you wouldn't know it if you saw him. To most people passing him walking his dog or waiting in line at Kroger down the street from his house, he was just another schlepper, wearing a faded baseball hat, a pair of worn jeans, an ordinary jacket that zipped up and maybe a crazy tie that sat kind of cockeyed under his shirt collar, as if he couldn't be bothered to put it on right.

After his funeral, someone told a Boo story. It seems a police officer was cruising through an alley behind Gaston Street. They were looking for some miscreant and thought they found him when they came across Boo. Questioned by the officer about why he was there, Boo said, "Well, officer, I'm just taking the garbage out of my house like I've done for the past 70 years."

When Boo passed away he was 82. Because of Hurricane Dorian

and the decision to close Bonaventure Cemetery before the storm hit Savannah, he was buried a day earlier than planned, in front of a fraction of the number of people who would have been there if they had not evacuated—because people loved Boo, many people. They loved his down-to-earth, old-world ways. Several people new to town mentioned that Boo never failed to say hello or to welcome them. Sadly, that doesn't always happen when newcomers move into an established neighborhood.

They say we can't talk to the dead after they're gone, but in this case at least, we can listen to them. Thanks to the foresight of the City of Savannah's Ellis Square Oral History Project, we can hear Boo, clear as day, tell his stories. It's rich listening and available to all. He talks about the time in 1943 when his mother walked him to the Massie School for his first day of school. When she left, a little teary-eyed, the six-year-old Boo waited a little while before he scooted out the front door. "They found me on Broughton Street watching the tanks and guns roll down the street. It was a bond drive and they were raising money for the war. My first day of school and I became a truant, something I—sadly—did the rest of my life."

He talked about walking to the "big park"—what Savannahians call Forsyth Park—and buying peanuts from the "peanut man," and about his father who was chief clerk of the city's Department of Public Works. He remembers walking to City Market with his grandfather, who came to town from Eastern Europe because the Jewish community needed a shochet (to butcher meat according to the standards of a kosher diet) and a mohel (to perform circumcisions on newborn boys).

"It's so ironic," Boo said. "Such a gentle man doing these things. I thought, 'How can he do that?' but there were so many Jewish families that kept kosher, someone had to. At the end of his day, he'd go to the synagogue on Montgomery Street (now the home of SCAD's student center) or to the Alliance (an earlier name for the Jewish Educational Alliance) to read the paper, have his tea and play chess. He was a top-flight chess player.

"Papa was an amazing character with a beautiful heart and soul. I remember how irritated my mother would get seeing him leave the house with brown pants and a blue jacket. He would say, 'How else would people know I had two suits?'

"One Christmas Eve, I wanted Santa Claus to come like he did for all the Christian kids on the block. When my mother sought my grandfather's sage advice, he said, 'There's no law that says he can't believe in Santa Claus.' They got me a stocking and made a fire in the fireplace. But I went ballistic thinking Santa would climb down the chimney into a fire. Papa didn't know what to do. It was the Sabbath and you're not supposed to use the phone but he broke down and called my father. It was Christmas Eve and he was working late at our store, Hornstein's Market. My father told me, 'Don't worry. I left a note on the roof for Santa to come in the front door.'"

There were no names attached to who conducted the oral history project and that's too bad. But I agree with the narrator's final assessment: "That was one of the best interviews we've ever done."

With Boo Hornstein behind the mike, how could it not be?

9/22/19

9 / *Laura Devendorf*
(written nearly six years before her passing on February 10, 2020)

Let's see. She's an abstract painter, an art critic, an equestrian course designer, a noted historic preservationist, an outspoken and creative activist, an astute parser of legalese who could in another era have been a fine lawyer. She's also an environmental steward, a tree farmer, an interior designer, a restorer of vernacular architecture, the owner of a piece of property that's been in her family's hands since England's King George II (granted to them in 1755), a relative of Thomas Jefferson (who was her fifth great-grandfather on her mother's side), the great-granddaughter of a Savannah mayor, a wag of the first order, and a native Savannahian who grew up in the era of crisp linens, white kid gloves and out-of-town boarding schools.

What could possibly be left for Laura Devendorf to do?

Can you say: write a book?

Laura insists *Killing with Kindness,* a collection of short stories, is fiction "modified by the clarity gained through time and by the creative needs of the stories." She writes, "Names and locations have been changed and characters should not be presumed to be people you know, even though your private experiences make them seem so." Sixteen years after starting this book, Laura is ready to put it out to the world and she's got some stories to tell.

Consider this: Here's a woman who grew up in the residential, historic neighborhood of Ardsley Park, went to The Pape School (which morphed into Savannah Country Day), was shuttled off to the boarding school du jour, did the whole coming-out thing, and then, with characteristic Laura Devendorf moxie, chose for her college years the University of Wisconsin, one of the country's most progressive public schools, a state-centered university that accepted only one hundred and fifty out-of-state students in an enrollment of eighteen thousand.

Yes, Laura, now 82, was smart. But mainly she was contrary.

"I was a rebel, a maverick," she said. "There would be no lady ivy school for me. My father was scandalized at my choice. This was not my destiny."

The school was tough ("chastening"), academically rigorous, a jolt for the Savannah freshman who described herself in the book as a "sad Southern troglodyte." She finished a year, wrote for the Daily Cardinal, the school newspaper, then sprang back to her native city to marry, have a few children, get divorced, meet someone new from New York and move to San Francisco for another couple dozen colorful chapters that included neighbors such as Carlos Santana, Janis Joplin and members of Blood, Sweat & Tears.

By this time she was taking what she learned from David Reese at the Telfair Art School in the late '50s—and from designing sets for the Junior League with the late Danny Zarem—and turning it into a career as an artist. After returning to her family's ten thousand-acre property in Liberty County, following the death of her parents (her father operated the successful Stevens Shipping Co.), she made another 180-degree turn and became an international equestrian course designer, one of a handful of women in the profession.

Decades later, after engaging in multiple confrontations, meetings and battles with Liberty County commissioners, state legislators, lobbyists and developers over her passion for cultural preservation and the environment, Laura credits the University of Wisconsin's Integrated Liberal Studies program, an interdisciplinary approach to learning, for aiding her activism and developing her philosophy.

"Everything is integrated," she said. "Politics, architecture, culture, history. You've got to be able to see all of these things happening in a certain time period."

In their fights to ward off intrusion by the state and to protect

Melon Bluff, the two thousand-acre nature preserve Laura owns and operates with her daughter, Meredith, the mother-daughter team knew they needed to do something consequential if they wanted their land to stay pristine and free of development. That's when they set up the Springfield Legacy Foundation, a consortium of the University of Georgia, the University of Western Florida, Seabrook Village and Sea Grant, an oceanic research operation. Meredith has a master's degree in environmental management and is working on a doctorate in the environmental history of the Georgia coast.

The foundation they formed, Laura said, is more airtight than most land trust programs.

"If you're going to do this work, you've got to do your homework and look around the corners," she said. "Most people are passionate for about a year, but if you're going to be prepared you've got to get on your hands and knees."

Without skipping a beat, this storyteller nonpareil turned the conversation in another direction.

"Oh, did I tell you I have two brain tumors? One was found twenty-six years ago, the other one two years ago. Well, I can't get all fists to furrowed brow about it. But the cyber knife they use: it's like a giant oil rig. That's another story. You live with what you have. I really think overall I'm very lucky."

10/6/14

10 / Mary O'Brien

In February, Mary O'Brien drove to a gathering in Rock Hill, South Carolina, to meet and hear the words of Edwina Gateley, a lightning rod, a radical, a social activist from Chicago. After the speech—held amongst a gathering of Catholic clergy—O'Brien bought Gateley's latest book, *A Warm Moist Salty God: Women Journeying Toward Wisdom.*

In the book, Gately writes, "For Mary, I can see God in your eyes."

A quick study, this Edwina Gateley. Those words captured precisely who Mary O'Brien was.

As a stranger, Gateley couldn't have known anything about O'Brien, who passed away unexpectedly last Saturday morning at age 70. She has suffered a stroke Thursday night while on the phone with her daughter, Ann.

From her name, Gateley might have guessed at O'Brien's Irish Catholic background. But that's all. She wouldn't have known how conversant she was—or was not—in the ways of the church, how active or inactive she remained, how much she did or did not continue to believe.

She wouldn't have known about Tom and Mary O'Brien's house on Whitfield Avenue, the nine children (eight living), the thirteen grandchildren, the scores of first, second and third cousins. Neither did the rest of us. We knew Mary O'Brien, but not that one.

While nearly 500 people spilled out of Sacred Heart Catholic Church Monday night, men and women well acquainted with the earlier Mary O'Brien—the Mary O'Brien from her first communion, through grade school, through hours and hours spent in catechism and prayer—some of us newcomers knew her only outside the church.

We met her in a different phase of life, no less complete or passionate than the previous one, but perhaps more up to date, more current.

The Mary O'Brien we knew was moved by people like Sister Helen Prejean, the nun portrayed in the movie *Dead Man Walking*, which dramatized the inequities on death row.

The Mary O'Brien we met was impressed enough by the Buddhists she encountered traveling this country by foot, promulgating peace, that she herself went to Japan, where she stayed in monasteries to learn and absorb even more.

One relative said her passion for social justice began with a revelation during her first grandchild's baptism. "She looked around," said sister-in-law Alice O'Brien, "and decided she didn't like where the world was heading."

That grandchild is now 21.

Every spring, this simply and modestly dressed woman with the kind words, the big glasses and the pin showing a picture of the Earth and the words, "All one people," would join a group from Savannah on their way to Fort Benning, the U.S. Army base near Columbus.

Their mission? To protest alleged terrorist training at the School of the Americas—now called the Western Hemisphere Institute for Security Cooperation.

I can only imagine what some of her family or church friends must have felt seeing Mary's picture on the front page of the newspaper when she was arrested for her beliefs. By then, they must have realized that the person they knew in their youth—this mild-mannered capable woman of the 1950s, conventional, traditional, proper—was heading in some entirely new direction, with an entirely different moral compass as her guide.

But knowing Mary—who was not one to proselytize, criticize or pass judgment—I think she probably gave those people plenty of space and a wide enough berth to catch up and jump on.

Her life set a high bar.

She did her part. Now the rest is up to us.

5/14/03

QUENTIN CRISP ON TRAIN TRAVEL

"I like traveling by rail. It is a situation in which no one can blame you for doing absolutely nothing but looking out of the window for several hours."

ROAD TRIPPING

1 / *In South Haven, Michigan with a 10-week-old (Go in good health)*

A tooth disorder is no way to start a road trip, especially when the dentist sends you off with a three-part package: two packets of cement, the tiniest of brushes to apply the cement and one of those nasty white cylindrical cotton things that make you gag. "Just in case the temporary falls out," he says of the glue.

How did this happen?

I already know about crowns coming off when I'm miles away from the home dentist. I also know about using toothpaste to make the interim repair. Now I have special glue.

"We're falling apart," said Susan, a friend in Nashville, after drawing our attention to three sets of feet, all crossed at the knees, all sporting Band-Aids on various toes, all with various stages of hammertoe.

We don't care. We have our cement. We have our Band-Aids. We have each other. That night in Nashville, never at a loss for great music, we go to the Family Wash, a retrofitted laundromat in an obscure neighborhood, to hear Amelia White. Our feet don't hurt and a beer or two never did dislodge or disturb a tooth.

One day and some five hundred miles later, in a cottage in South Haven, Michigan, I'm holding Lily, a two-week-old baby with ten perfect toes, nothing hammered there, nothing out of place. She has two miniature feet whose soft, silky bottoms have yet to touch the earth, and no teeth to decay, replace, restore or repair.

She breathes deeply from her diaphragm, too. It's picture-perfect, just the way we're supposed to breathe, her whole body shifting when she takes and releases a breath. No ADVAIR for her. No asthma-relieving medicine for Lily.

We're sitting on the screened porch of a modest cottage that a group of early Jewish immigrants from Eastern Europe who settled in Chicago built for their families to spend their summers. Nothing fancy. The roads are still not paved. Many of the houses, this one in particular, still lack air-conditioning.

Lily is the fourth generation of her family to stay in the cottage. She's the great-granddaughter of Sylvia and Henry, the grandchild of Rae, the daughter of Rebecca, the niece of Zander. We are awed by this.

With no television connection and no desire to listen to radio chatter, we take a break from world news and crowd onto the porch, presumably the coolest spot, although this summer, with temperatures in the high 90s in Michigan, the words "cool" and "spot" together are an oxymoron.

It's amazing how little we talk of politics, of global warming, of the Middle East. We have The Nation, the New Yorker and today's newspaper. Instead we joke about the National Enquirer that I bought as a joke.

Is it because of the baby? I wonder. Are we shielding her virgin ears from the contamination of mankind, from what lies ahead for her, from toothaches to pending war? Are we using her as an excuse, a diversion? Certainly, we could talk about Israel. We all have lots of views about Israel and they're not all the same. We could rehash Iraq. We could rehash Bush. We've done it before. We'll do it again. But not now. Not when she's so innocent and clean and fresh. There's time for that.

At night, after the sun finally sets, somewhere around 10 p.m., a few of us walk to the lift, a curious open box of an elevator. It's operated by a series of pulleys, not unlike a ski lift. We put in the key and descend through the trees, past the bluff (which has a stairway with 112 steps, depending on who's counting) to Lake Michigan. There's a sign on the lift, a Yiddish word, gei gezundter heit (go away in good health), followed by the name of a rather lofty-sounding organization:

MPSTA, the Mt. Pleasant Subdivision Transit Authority). The half-moon casts a tunnel of light on the water, uncharacteristically warm. Still, we have to keep an eye on one another. There are waves, even in a lake.

Back at the cottage, refreshed, revived, I ask for the baby. I ask for Lily. This is her "up" time. It all goes well for a while. Then on my watch, always my watch, while the mother and father take a well-earned walk, she starts to wail.

"Stick your finger in her mouth," someone tells me.

Stick my finger in her mouth? Are you sure? She's sure. Since my hands are clean—I've already been told more than once, "Wash your hands if you're going to pick up the baby"—I do as instructed. I slide my finger into her mouth. It works. She latches on—that's a breast-feeding term, I learn later. She goes to work. She settles down. No teeth but she's got some mighty strong gums.

Someone comes back with news from the Middle East. She's been watching television at a neighbor's cottage. The world is falling apart, she says. But we don't pick up the bait. We don't respond, other than to say, Shh. Lily's sleeping. We'll talk of war later.

8/27/06

2 / A wedding in Israel
(Belly dancers and crutches)

It doesn't hurt the narrative if it's a destination wedding (in Israel), if the cheapest way to get there is to fly on a Russian airline (Aeroflot), or if our first few days in the country were spent with friends in East Jerusalem who live across the street from Pope Francis' Jerusalem residence, BYU Jerusalem Center and an Israeli settlement, all within earshot of the 4:30 a.m. Muslim call to prayer (during Ramadan).

Sometimes it takes more luck than brains, said my Detroit-born cousin Beth, the mother of the bride, using one of her favorite Hebrew expressions. She was referencing being able to find a parking spot near a beloved shawarma dive in the 24-hour, car-crazed, Bauhaus-heavy, global city of Tel Aviv where the biggest thing to fear, according to Beth, is a traffic accident.

But she might have been referencing our luck when we told her about leaving the Old City and asking the cab driver to find us a wine shop, which he did on some dark and twisty street. Leaving the motor running and the radio going ("Girls Just Want to Have Fun"), he dashed into the shop to facilitate the sale. None for him, though. It was Ramadan. He was Muslim.

Or maybe Beth was thinking about our luck when we started talking about visits to the Palestinian/Muslim-populated Bethlehem and Jericho, all places on the other side of the unpopular check points within the contested West Bank that are not that easy for Israeli Jews to visit. We passed the controversial Israeli West Bank barrier, decorated by some crazy graffiti, including some by Banksy, the English political activist and graffiti artist. My favorite? "Make hummus not war." We stopped and walked in Wadi Qelt, an eerie desert landscape between Jerusalem and Jericho where a sixth-century Greek monastery is tucked into the cliffs. We didn't see any monks and we resisted buying trinkets from a bedouin who approached on his donkey. Somewhere near the Dead Sea we stopped for gas and stared at a camel and camel driver who were resting in the shade.

In a country the size of New Jersey it's pretty crazy to think of all the people (listed in no particular order) who have traveled/owned/ lived/claimed parts of the land: the Etruscans, the Romans, the Christians, the Muslims, Napoleon, the Mamluks, the Jews, the Arabs, the Turks, the Brits. Even Mark Twain chimed in with his book *The Innocents Abroad*. That's how I felt in this Middle East conundrum, like an innocent, an amateur, an observer.

And that was before my feet tangled in a mass of wire in Tel Aviv and I fell, smack on the knee, somewhere on the street that parallels the Mediterranean Sea. All that was before I got back to Savannah to find out I had broken my kneecap.

But life goes on. After "The Fall" (and a full day on my back, watching Wimbledon in Hebrew with occasional Russian subtitles and Israeli beach soccer and, in between, multiple icings and pain pills) and before "The Immobilizer," a full-length black knee brace I would get in Savannah to keep the knee stiff so it can heal (can you say the hollow-legged Dennis Weaver as Chester in "Gunsmoke"?), there was "The Wedding." Guests came from Romania, Thailand, Minneapolis, Seattle, Flint, Detroit, Argentina, New York City, Washington, D.C., and Boston.

Using my Israeli crutches and traveling in a golf cart arranged by the congenial Avner, the bride's father (like that's all he had to do), I followed 250 guests and a New Orleans-style jazz band up a hill in the old port city of Jaffa to beautiful early evening skies to see Hadar and Sheldon and their family under the traditional huppa, the portable white canopy symbolizing the future home of the newlyweds. And then the dancing began. Some of us kept time with the rubber tips of our crutches. The bride's sister donned a belly-dancing outfit. Everyone did the hora. Someone else Skyped the whole wedding ceremony and party in real time to the groom's grandfather, who lives in San Diego. We got back to the hotel at 2:30 a.m.

Trips rarely turn out the way you expect them to. Instead of floating in the Dead Sea and smearing myself with mud, I schmoozed with cousins and their children. Instead of revisiting Yad Vashem, the memorial to the victims of the Holocaust, I ate leftovers from The Wedding with other out-of-towners. Instead of returning to Jerusalem, I piled into a car with everyone else, drove to the Mediterranean Sea and on July Fourth watched the sunset.

I left the country with a lot of questions, a bum knee, and a full heart.

7/12/15

3 / Germany makes amends
(And owns its past)

Say what you want about visiting Europe.

I know I did.

"Let's go somewhere else," I complain in typical First World, privileged, entitled, whining fashion when trying to decide where to vacation during these long summer days and nights.

What about Utah? Or Vietnam? Or South Africa? We settle on a quirky site-specific cultural festival in Terschelling. That's a barrier island in the North Sea off the Netherlands, where bikes are the major mode of transportation and installations include an old Volkswagen filled with water—and people. The artist calls it "Carpool." Where there was a midnight concert in the evocative sand dunes with dancers, choreographed lighting and the lone sound of a French horn off in the distance; and a happening in another pocket of sand dunes, where a woman dressed in a flowing gown played a grand piano.

It was nice to be on a bike, except it's not easy sharing a six-foot-wide bike lane with hundreds of Dutch people—young and old (lots of old)—riding behind you, in front of you and past you (mostly past you), people who were born on bikes and could probably balance their checkbooks, make a complicated airline reservation and conduct an intimate conversation at the same time, if challenged.

They are good at this biking thing. "Speed is your friend," one helpful rider offers as he passes us, advice meant only to help not to harm. They are only kind (and tall), these engineering-prone and ingenious Dutch who have reclaimed much of their land from the sea.

Alas, most do not wear helmets when they ride. P.S.: I didn't see one accident (well, maybe one, and she was an American).

Before the festival, there's Amsterdam. It's drizzling. It's damp. The narrow room we booked on a houseboat is like a cell with two sets of bunk beds. But forget visiting the Anne Frank House. The line is a mile long. Nothing to do but go to a coffeeshop, which in the Netherlands has come to mean an alcohol-free establishment where cannabis is sold and consumed, all taxed, all regulated, all on the up and up, not unlike a handful of places in the States.

We did not fit the prototype, which might be why we were so well taken care of. "Everything OK?" the "bartender" signaled with a thumbs-up gesture and a smile. I believe we raised the average customer age threefold. It might have been the only place on the continent where European soccer wasn't being televised.

Say what you want about visiting Europe. They have the transportation thing down. (Just don't go wandering into the bike lane. You'll get mowed down.) The trains are comfortable and on time. The buses are double-decker. The taxis are cheap. The metro system is easy to follow. But best of all is a variation of car-sharing called Drive-Now. First, you download the app. Then when you need to get somewhere, you check a map on your phone for the nearest available car. When you find it, you punch in the magic numbers, open the door, drive to your destination, find a parking space and exit the car. You are charged by the minute, which is the only downside, our Savannah and Hamburg friend Imke told us. People tend to drive too fast.

Say what you want about visiting Germany. I know I did. Plenty. *I'm never going there*, I've said for decades. While I didn't lose any relatives to the Holocaust, plenty of other people did. I'll never buy a Volkswagen either, I said. But then I went. To visit Imke in Hamburg. And to visit another friend in Berlin. To see what it looks like when a country decides to remember victims of the Nazi regime, when a country decides to remember, not brush under the rug, its atrocities, when it's mandatory for school children to study the Holocaust.

In Berlin, we would see the Memorial to the Murdered Jews of Europe, an uneasy and eerie five-acre site of two thousand, seven hundred eleven concrete slabs arranged in a grid fashion and resembling a cemetery. It was confusing and disorderly, which is exactly what American architect Peter Eisenman was going for. There are no names on the slabs. Each one seems to be a different height and width. It's abstract, gray, disorienting and effective.

In Hamburg, Imke told us about the Stumbling Stones project. For this, a Berlin artist, Gunter Demnig, decided to place a square cobblestone-size brass plate in front of the homes of people who were wrenched away and sent to certain death in the concentration camps. The person's name and dates of birth, deportation and death are engraved into the brass plate, along with the words, "Here lived ... ". The artist has said he feels it's up to the younger generation in Germany to keep the memories alive. Unlike a conscious decision to visit a memorial, people have to "stumble" across the bricks, Demnig has said. He wants the decentralized memorial to intrude into everyday life so the memory of the atrocities can be kept alive. There are some fifty thousand stumbling stones in eighteen European countries. Each stone is manufactured by hand.

Say what you want about Germany or what happened when its people fell for a monster like Hitler. This is a country that has decided to own its despicable history. Do you think Savannah could learn a thing or two about its relationship to slavery to make sure something like that never happens again? I do.

7/9/16

4 / *A rendezvous in Paris*
(Hey, Julie,
are you up there?)

I was looking for tennis player Serena Williams. Instead I found singer Julie Rose Wilde. That's Paris. Not a bad trade. Serena, citing anonymity, likes to practice there. Julie, always looking to step up her musical game, thought Paris would be a great place to make an album. I wanted to practice my French, drink red wine without sulfites and see the Musée d'Orsay, once a grand railroad station, today a grand museum.

(Hey, Julie, are you there?)

I wanted to get lost in this café society of *liberté, égalité* and *fraternité*. Which I did, somewhere on the No. 4 Métro line, on the way to find Julie. Lost in the "camera roll" of my phone.

"I take you there," said a kindly conductor after the train stopped and everyone else had departed. No attitude. He backed up a stop, watched us get off the platform and smiled.

Then I took another gamble. In front of Julie's rented apartment on Rue Mouton-Duvernet. I spotted an open door on the second-floor balcony in this city of decorative wrought-iron balconies and spoke her name. "Julie?" No one should mind. There's always a buzz in Paris. People linger. In the cafes. At the markets. In glassed-in patios. They plot. They talk. They hook their pocketbooks, hats or canes on a clasp under the bar and stay awhile. No one hassles you to leave.

It worked. She heard me. Paris is a big city, two-and-a-half million, but few buildings are taller than four stories, by design. They care about proportions. They appreciate aesthetics.

Julie and collaborator Austin Smith were putting the final touches on "Mystery of Love in Paris," a big band, gypsy, jazzy album matching Julie's compositions and voice, Austin's orchestration, and the strings, horns and talents of twenty-seven local musicians.

"I feel like I'm in a dream," said Julie, who lives on Isle of Hope, another dream. "I'm sitting in the Hector Berlioz School of Music, laying down tracks, doing the overdubs and making this happen."

Believe it. This woman can make things happen. She recorded her last album in Nashville, then went to Paris to promote it. She sang with street bands and in a cabaret near the Moulin Rouge. She raised funds on an Austin-produced Indiegogo for a Kickstarter campaign where Julie sings in a dynamite black dress, black gloves and red rose. She secured quarters in Paris. And that's when she called Austin from Notre-Dame de Paris and said, "You have to be here."

"It's been in my mind forever," Julie said, "to go to Paris and sing."

There were a few chapters that came first.

Like Garden City, where Julie grew up, where her father was the fire chief. Like West 36th Street, where she and her sister took piano lessons. Like Georgia Southern University, where she earned undergraduate and graduate degrees after skipping 12th grade at Groves High School.

In and around music there was her downtown shop, Native Secrets, and her current jobs as a vocal coach to some twenty students, and an interior designer for the Kessler Collection hotels, including the Mansion on Forsyth Park.

But there's always been music. She taught for eight years in Savannah schools, then lived in Atlanta to work in a musical theater. At an American Traditions workshop in Savannah, she met a teacher from Los Angeles, where she went for more training. There was a teacher and more training in New York City Now there is her own group, Bohemian Dream Band.

Before arriving in Paris, Julie was armed with guitar parts from guitarist Bill Smith, Austin's father. When she and Austin needed a guitarist at the last minute, they engaged a prominent bassist, Biréli Lagrène, who lives near Strasbourg. When they needed more strings, they secured a well-known French jazz violinist, Didier Lockwood.

"I can't help myself," Julie said. "This is who I am. I'm always thinking, 'Wouldn't it be great if we, well, you know…'" she said, her voice trailing off. "I just love the process. I just think you have to take risks."

For me, the only thing left to do on my last day in Paris was to go hear some jazz on a late Sunday afternoon. We took the Métro to La Chope des Puces, a club on Rue des Rosiers, where Django Reinhardt used to live. As at all French gatherings there were kids, old people, young people (all wearing rakish scarves, of course). The guitarists, including Ninine Garcia, were polished, casual. They had a following. But I couldn't help wishing that a jazz singer from Isle of Hope was out there fronting the duo, offering a little swing, a little soul, a little mystery.

1/12/14

5 / *It's better to be seen than viewed (No one blinks at change)*

The question floated out of my mouth in all sincerity.

"That's Che?" I asked about seeing a photo of a friend's son in one of those personalized calendars people make of their family. "He looks so adult."

I was visiting friends in the Ozarks, where I lived a thousand years ago. The redbuds were in their prime, their purple plumes brightening the otherwise bare winter limbs. I didn't remember their utter beauty. Maybe they're having a comeback. The dogwoods and forsythia had finished their show for the year. I was too early (or was it too late?) for the lilacs, but I did catch the end of the daffodil dance.

I didn't need a sign—"crooked and steep for the next 6.5 miles" —to remind me of the twisty, turny mountain switchbacks on the highway to Eureka Springs, Arkansas, from the airport in Bentonville, past the Kum and Go and the Kozy Korner and through Gateway (pop. 405), but I could have used a warning about the traffic in Bentonville. Was I back in Pooler?

It's all Walmart related, of course. Billions of dollars later, the homegrown company with good organizational skills has transformed a sleepy part of northwest Arkansas, traffic included, starting with Alice Walton's Moshe Safdie-designed museum, *Crystal Bridges Museum of American Art*. Turns out Sam Walton's daughter has taste, drive and money.

Now two more Walton heirs, Tom and Steuart, are about to open another museum in a former Kraft Foods cheese factory with a "fermentation room" in a windowless space of brick, concrete and stainless steel, where artists are to be let loose to create whatever they want.

Too bad no one could anticipate the traffic cluster or the growth of the area, as anyone trying to catch a 10 a.m. flight would experience while you creep along with a ton of Walmart execs crawling to work along US 62. Many of them are headed to one of the largest distribution centers in the world, a space that covers more than 1.2 million square feet and that turns over ninety percent of its content in twenty-four hours.

But come on, no one can think—or remember—everything.

"You say he looks adult?" my friend responded when I commented on his son. "Maybe it's because he's approaching 40."

That's the way it is when you visit friends, revisit memories, pop into town, when you're busy doing other things yourself. Your mind can't keep up—even if you think otherwise. You're having a late-night pizza at Chelsea's when you think, "Didn't this used to be Sweet Dreams bakery?" Before you can fully remember, someone else says, "Yes, it was. And before that it was Rae's String Shop." Then there's Brews, a hip pub/art gallery/community gathering spot across from the post office at the foot of Pine Street where there used to be a giant buckeye tree. "Wasn't this the Assemblies of God church?" I say, taking a stab at history. "Yes," someone answers, "and then it became the Bell Museum." Right again.

Then there's Small World, a chic kids' shop of goodies that used to be called Pastimes. Except the name changed a couple of years ago, which I forgot. ("Why didn't anyone tell me?" I ask the owner, a friend of forty-plus years). Except then it moved ("Did I know that?"). Now it occupies the old deli that used to sit next to my old restaurant, the Pita Hut.

None of this is new to anyone but me. Everyone else has kept up, made the changes in their address book, their phone directory, their mental file box. Everyone has gone on to other things. The Walmart dynasty is old hat. The new stores, the old locations, a newcomer named Pearl are now seamlessly part of the fabric, which was good then and is good today. Now, two women who might have had little in common twenty years ago find themselves sharing a couple of grand-children. One woman who did everyone's astrological charts—big in the '70s—when she wasn't throwing artful pots went on to become a life coach and is now thinking about introducing laughing yoga to people with disabilities.

Another friend is headed to the Edamame Festival in Mulberry, Arkansas, to stump for a political candidate. Edamame, as in soybeans? Yep. They grow edamame in Arkansas? Yes, they do. First state in the country to try it.

No one blinks at any of these changes. Why would they? They live them.

No one blinks at any of our changes, either.

"It's so good to see you," we say, answered by, "It's better to be seen than viewed," followed by, "You look just the same." And while that—let's face it—might not be altogether true, to us, deep inside, it is true. We who have known one another for multiple decades, through good times and bad times, look at who is in front of us and see our younger selves—and that's a beautiful thing.

4/14/18

6 / *Topiary Artist*
in Bishopville
(It looks so easy; it's not)

There's a man in Bishopville, South Carolina, who breaks all the rules. He's an artist with no training. He's a sculptor who chops up yews, saws around hollies and clips up privet. He's a late bloomer, an outsider. He's a visionary, an absurdist, a surrealist who has transformed the three acres surrounding his ordinary red-brick ranch home on an ordinary dead-end street into a dreamland, a moonscape, a garden fit for the Jetsons. It could be an English garden of angles and clean lines except none of what he creates makes any sense. There is no balance. The lines go this way and that way. Out of the towering trees, there are geometric shapes, animal facsimiles (could that be two bears hugging?) and sudden holes. Lots of holes. There is negative space.

After forty years of working his magic in what was once a cornfield, this generous, gregarious, community-minded man has attracted enough attention and money to be able to form a nonprofit organization that hands out scholarships, but only to students with C grade averages.

He's a Will Allen of gardening, a Howard Finster of junk sculptures, a peace-and-love kind of guy who helped desegregate the lunch counters in Durham, North Carolina, where he was majoring in mathematics and chemistry at North Carolina Central University (anything to escape the sharecropping farm life of his family, he once said).

He's Pearl Fryar, and he's just as accessible as the cook behind the counter at the local Waffle House on Main Street, where he takes his breakfast every day and where one of his twisty, loopy, circular plant sculptures stands. He's as passionate with the kids he talks to as he is about the creatures he creates out of his trees.

Lead with your strength, he tells them. Be patient. Find what you're good at. And when you get successful, he says, take someone with you from the bottom. Make a difference.

You can't miss his garden. Somewhere past a stretch of highways noting the birthplace of Althea Gibson (good to see the name of the late, great African American tennis player in print; she was born some forty miles away from here to parents who worked as sharecroppers on a cotton farm), past the John Deere outlet which also has one of Fryar's whirlygig creations (maybe it was a loblolly pine or a compacted holly), not far from Harry & Harry Too restaurant (closed on Saturday), where you'll see a small sign with yet another of his otherworldly pieces of art pointing toward his house.

There's no fee to visit his garden (contributions are welcome). There's no uniformity to the five hundred plants of his fertile imagination. Many would call what he does topiary, but Fryar doesn't use armature or wire cages. He doesn't water or fertilize. He just trims and trims until the surface is tight, not unlike what AstroTurf looks like or a finely cut putting green. Fryar didn't know anything about topiaries when he visited a nursery some forty years ago and asked someone how to shape a plant. It looked interesting, he thought, followed by, "I'd like to do that."

"Three minutes," Fryar told us. "That's how long the man talked before he gave me a few plants out of the compost pile. It's a good thing, too. If I would have had a horticulture background or known any more, I would not have been able to do this."

Fryar, 76, went to college, moved up north, served in the military, got a job with a can manufacturing company and married his high school sweetheart who worked in a sunglasses factory. When the company built a new plant in Bishopville, he and his family transferred south, albeit with a union wage and a union salary. After working twelve-hour shifts, Fryar would come home, set up his thirty-foot ladders and "cut his bushes" late into the night. That's how he likes to describe what he does: "In the final analysis, that's what I do: I cut my

bushes." He had one immediate goal: "to win Yard of the Month."
One thing is for sure, he told us, "I was not going to do what anyone
else was doing."

Now he's the subject of a movie, "A Man Named Pearl." He talks
about the creative process at local colleges. His touch is everywhere,
including four-foot words cut into his yard—"peace," "love," "good
will" and his street number, "165," in front of his house. Then there
are Fryar's neighbors on his street. They couldn't help themselves.
They started cutting up their own bushes. Fryar doesn't mind. "They
do it themselves," he says. "Fine with me."

Everyone in town seems to know him. At Watford's Bar B Que
restaurant, where peacock feathers top the Christmas tree, the wait-
ress (who has a farm with peacocks, hedgehogs and ratites) sells 2016
Fryar calendars.

"Tell him I sold you two," she says when we leave.

1/3/16

7 / *Martinis in Molena*
(and a Reuben
from the Mennonites)

Don't you love it when you're standing around at a Chinese New Year's party, holding a glass of wine, celebrating the Year of the Rat, when someone who eschews small talk puts you on the spot and asks how many Georgia state representatives or senators you can name?

Not too many, as it turns out. They all sounded familiar when he listed them (I never was good at recall; recognition, better). Still, a pretty embarrassing moment. Does it count if I said I watched some interviews from the State Capitol, in Atlanta, on Georgia Public Broadcasting? Probably not. For the record, Georgia has one hundred eighty state representatives and fifty-six senators. We read all kinds of conspiracy theories into city council meetings, we tear out our hair about national politics (can you say every morning?). But at the state level? Very little awareness.

I felt just as clueless last week when I visited some friends in the Piedmont—far from Savannah—somewhere between the Blue Ridge Mountains and the Coastal Plain. As it turns out people there talk, they laugh, they think, they read, they argue, they paint, they sculpt, they write, they gossip, they pay attention when the sandhill cranes migrate (way too early), they worry about streams and rivers from the Flint River overflowing their banks (all this rain). They note that mowing the lawn in February is just not right (nature is confused).

It's nice to get out of town, especially when you choose Greyhound instead of a car to meet a friend in Atlanta for the drive to parts west and southwest. For the occasion, I wore a The Grey Market hat with a nice drawing of a greyhound (the dog, not the bus) and read *Grounded: A Down to Earth Journey Around the World*, by Seth Stevenson, an intrepid reporter for Slate. He wrote the book about circumnavigating the world without once taking to the air. Brave man. Good reporting.

On its way to downtown Atlanta and the Atlanta airport, the bus from Savannah makes one short stop—in Macon, not far from the Georgia Sports Hall of Fame and a bench crowded with people who look as if they have taken up residency. It's a no-nonsense ride. At the beginning, the bus driver announces he will not tolerate any profanity, smoking in the bathroom, people "extending their legs in the aisle or sneezing without covering their mouth." The seats were roomy, the shocks substantial, the bus on time. He warned against cell phones ringing.

Traffic is light west of Atlanta. Schools are named after Robert E. Lee and Jeff Davis. Isolated brick chimneys from sharecroppers' homes dot the landscape. So does the occasional sharecropper cabin, still standing. Daffodils, just as yellow as can be but shorter than ours, are already up. Sprawling, defunct mills sit empty. There are more Dollar Generals than Starbucks.

There are artists, writers, pontificators, too. A friend in Molena (pop. 475, Pike County) who makes a good martini and a tasty chocolate chip cookie runs a popular fine arts photo gallery (South x Southeast) in a barn on her great-great-grandparents' farm. In a downtown Greenville (pop. 946, Meriwether County) art gallery, artist Annie Greene, 88, offers an extraordinary show of yarn art, not too far away from Sandra Miller, still producing pottery in her upper 80s.

In Yatesville (pop. 347, Upson County), Anna Lee's, a chic, trendy and under-the-radar junk store, sits close enough to Atlanta to attract people from all over the world who fly into Atlanta to rent a car and drive through "the old South."

In between galleries there's a stellar Reuben sandwich on rye at the Country Cupboard and Deli in Thomaston (Upson County). The restaurant and bakery are run by folks from the Mennonite community who came from Montezuma (that's in Macon County). The chicken salad sandwich on toasted homemade sourdough bread is a close second.

A more well-known attraction is Franklin Delano Roosevelt's six-room, one-story Little White House in Warm Springs (Meriwether County). FDR consciously built a house like others in the area. It's simple, modest and humble, a reminder of a more thoughtful, compassionate and caring time in Washington, D.C.

For the record, none of these places is in Savannah, Athens or Atlanta. It's good to get out from under the bubble.

2/22/20

8 / Pie in DeValls Bluff, Arkansas (Banana cream pie and men with earrings)

You leave home with a newly patched rotten roof you should have addressed months ago (*maybe it won't get any worse*, you think; let's hear it for denial), a weakened and collapsed ceiling in the back room of the house (situated under said rotten roof), a Rube Goldberg arrangement of stools and ladders holding up the remains of aforementioned collapsed ceiling until your worker can get to it, and curse your terrible timing. But you go ahead anyway with your plans to leave town, which have already been waylaid three times because life, it seems, can get in the way of, well, life. You assign chicken care, cat sitting and vermicomposting duties to a couple of generous neighbors, sweep the floors, clean the porch, put away the dishes, leave a few lights on, pack the newly serviced car with multiple pairs of shoes (you never know) and remember to take one of those oversize and old-fashioned Rand McNally road atlases for the all-important overview.

It's not always easy to get the heck out of Dodge.

But it's necessary. How else to finish Leo Tolstoy's *Anna Karenina*, an 800-page book started on another road trip four years ago. This is a challenging way to continue reading such a long book—even with a cheat sheet from Wikipedia to keep track of a dozen major characters you've already forgotten—but it's strangely in sync with the way the book was originally published. Over a four-year period—from 1873 to 1877—a periodical published Tolstoy's masterpiece in serial installments. Now, as it must have been then, it was worth waiting for the next episode. The man can write.

Spoiler alert: The book does not end well for the title charac-ter. Somewhere around the time we were crossing the Arkansas del-ta and searching out Ms. Lena's Pie Shop in DeValls Bluff, Arkansas, Tolstoy's Anna faced the railroad tracks and ended her misery, Levin had his come-to-Jesus moment and we were sitting in the car eating a piece of banana cream pie, a gift ("put your money away") of Viv Barnhill, the late Ms. Lena's daughter, even though it was a Tuesday and the shop was closed, except there she was, sitting on a concrete step, smoking a cigarette, baking a pie for her brother-in-law, who was visiting in a few hours.

Lucky us. That, along with a $4 watermelon bought in town and plans to recreate a cold cucumber gazpacho soup we ate at The Grey Market, brought us to our destination: a visit with old friends in north-west Arkansas. Our friendships have only grown richer. With a history of laughing together, traveling together, dreaming and growing up to-gether, now we have a basis for talking about aging and dying parents, about half-brothers and -sisters who show up unannounced through DNA testing, about news of an African-American grandfather who passed as white and would mysteriously disappear to visit his "other," darker family. We talk of wonky knees, cancer scares, cancer battles, cancer tests.

While it's true the more things change, the more they stay the same, this part of the country is not the same lily-white place I moved to on a whim some forty years ago.

Back then, there was the beauty of the Ozarks, but no one grow-ing grapes utilized the electronic sound of distressed birds to scare away other birds. No one could visit a world-class museum, the Crys-tal Bridges Museum of American Art, in Bentonville, Arkansas. This is the brainchild of Alice Walton. Walton, daughter of Walmart's Sam Walton, loves art, she loves American art, she loves seeking out un-known artists of color to whom she rewards thousands of dollars to show their art. Vanessa German, an artist from the Pittsburgh neigh-borhood of Homewood, is one of those artists. Titus Kaphar is another.

Last year the museum brought "Soul of a Nation: Art in the Age of Black Power," an exhibit developed by the Tate Modern, in London. It debuted for the first time in the U.S. at Crystal Bridges.

"Imagine that," a friend said. "Bentonville, Arkansas, and London in one sentence."

P.S.: There is no charge at Crystal Bridges—never, not just on holidays, not just on "Museum Sunday." To walk through this Moshe Safdie-designed museum, built into the rocks: It's free, always. That's a beautiful thing.

In Fayetteville, Arkansas, a college town of seventy-three thousand, some thirty thousand people marched down Dickson Street in the annual gay pride festival. That same week, Eureka Springs conceptual artist John Rankine opened an exhibit of photographs called "Men With Earrings."

Except for the drive around Atlanta (how do people live that way? The dull, monotonous Interstate 16 never looked so good), the drive home was rich with memories—and the end of Gabrielle Hamilton's book *Blood, Bones & Butter: The Inadvertent Education of a Reluctant Chef.*

During our time with old friends, we talked of moving here, moving there, doing this, doing that, but in the end all our conversations came back to one thing: "Wherever you go, there you are." By the time we got back to Dodge, the night was steamy, the chickens looked fine, and the Rube Goldberg arrangement was working.

6/30/19

9 / *We heard, we gathered, we marched (But did he hear?)*

Did he hear? That's the question. Or is it?

There we were, hundreds of people from Savannah at last week's Women's March in Washington D.C. We wielded colorful hand-painted signs, compliments of the generous, bighearted, kindhearted Panhandle Slim, Savannah's own iconic painter. We all traveled our own way. Post-Inauguration Day. We bused, flew, drove or took the train. Twenty-four hours later, when we left D.C., and disembarked on an early and rainy Sunday morning, a conductor on the Miami-bound Silver Meteor No. 97 passed through the dark and narrow aisle, cautioned us to take all our stuff, looked at the battered signs under our arms and asked the question.

"But do you think he heard; do you think the president heard?" She wasn't hostile; she was curious. She wasn't belligerent; she was, in fact, complimentary. "You all were the best-behaved group I've had all week."

I think we were just tired. For twelve hours, from the moment we got to D.C. at 7a.m. (the train arrived on time that morning because seats were sold out early on so there were fewer stops) until the time we left the jam-packed, drop-dead gorgeous Beaux-Arts station that evening we were bombarded with imagery, words, chants, faces, bodies, amateur paparazzi ("Can we take your picture?").

We heard instructions ("Call 202-225-3121 to talk to your representative in Congress every day," urged Michael Moore). We got reminders ("Don't get frustrated, get involved." This from Muhammad Ali's daughter). We got admonitions ("Sometimes pressing 'send' is not enough," warned Gloria Steinem). We heard words of wisdom from the still-fiery, still-wise Angela Davis, who reminded us, "We are agents of history; history cannot be deleted like web pages."

Yes, there were probably too many speeches (some forty-four listed in the original lineup, but I bet there were more. At some point, you just stop counting). Yes, some were better than others. Yes, I'm sorry I wiggled out of the scrum before seeing Cher (how often do you get to see Cher?). But to break free and walk down Pennsylvania Avenue, to hear the cheers from people standing on the balcony of the Newseum when the press is so maligned, to run into people (can you say: my neighbor with her two teenage girls?) or someone who recognized my Panhandle Slim sign, which meant I was from Savannah ("Do you know my friend Molly? Tell her hello for me!").

The speeches represented the meat of the matter. We teared up when the impressive and young R&B singer Janelle Monáe introduced us to mothers of young Black men who had been killed on the streets (think Trayvon Martin), when she introduced me and other comfortable, middle-class white women to a hipster call-and-response, African-American combination of words, pronounced "talmbout." This is when I say: Thank goodness for the online Urban Dictionary. Janelle would yell out "talmbout"—short for "(What the) hell (are) you talkin(g) about?" And we would return with the deceased man's name. That was powerful.

And the signs: so cool. "I can't believe we still have to protest this **** again." Or, "Computers took our jobs, not Mexicans. Learn how to use one."

It takes stamina—and bags of almonds and raisins—to stand hip to hip, shoulder to shoulder for four hours in a mosh pit as speakers deliver their take on the world as we know it. We got there early and had a good view of the speakers, set up somewhere between the curvy, stunning limestone Museum of Native American History and the gray, bureaucratic Rayburn House Office Building. People in the crowd were polite, but one thing soon became clear: No one was moving. This was not a place for claustrophobes.

We heard, we gathered, we marched

This was not my first march. There's the Vietnam War. The Iraq War. Women's rights. Gay rights. Equal rights. Before leaving, I appreciated the sentiment but found it curious when friends said, "Be safe." I never felt unsafe. Despite the media concentration on occasional incidents and the intensity of the subject, gatherings like this are more often than not peaceful and empowering. While you may not always feel you are among "your people" in everyday life—at the bank, the grocery store, the park—this time you know you are and that's profound. While it's helpful to have dialogue with people "on the other side," it's not always easy. It should be, but it's not.

At any moment I could look around the crowd and spot a teenager, an oldster on a walker, men, women, Black people, white people, babies on shoulders and feel as if I could weep. Odd, I know. But real. It wasn't so much the kumbaya moment as a feeling of camaraderie. It was heartening.

And then there were all those knitted cat-like pink hats. While some of us arrived with hats made by friends (and care packages of cheese, apples and bread), there were others giving hats away—free!—along with the knitter's name. They weren't even asking for money. The hat I snagged for a friend was made by "Lynn from Lansing, Mi."

When we got back to Savannah, two more Amtrak employees screamed in delight at our signs, clapped when they heard we saw Angela Davis and hugged us for going.

"But do you think he heard you?"

I doubt it. But we heard. We gathered. We marched. That's the important thing. For now.

1/28/17

10 / *When your cousin lives in B.C. (Hey, it's Canada)*

With a few sprigs of lavender stuck in my jean jacket pocket (lavender grows like a weed in British Columbia; those lucky dogs, though not as lucky at the plant-loving bees who have set up house there), I catch the 6:20 a.m. ferry in Horseshoe Bay, headed across a series of islands under the shadow of a snow-covered mountaintop for the mainland of Vancouver.

It's a five-minute drive downhill from my cousin Maggie's house on the Sunshine Coast, a cheesy name for a rugged part of the western Canadian coast accessible only by ferry. People who live here get used to watching for the ferry from the decks of their homes on the hills, then scurrying to their car for the quick downhill trip.

The ferry is crowded. It leaves on time. A hot breakfast is available. People who drive onto the boat stay in their car for the short ride across the strait, open a book and get a little reading done.

I'm leaving a family gathering including six children under age 10 and various and sundry adults related in all kinds of creative ways who live in Switzerland, central Chile (where they tend hectares and hectares of cherries, eighty percent of which are exported to China, a phenomenon of the last few years), Toronto, and Goleta, California. If you're wondering how to get your extended family together more often, move to British Columbia. It's not easy to get to; for me it was two flights, one city train, one bus, one ferry and the short uphill car ride.

That hasn't stopped people from visiting or moving there. Plenty of people from California have done just that. Warning: The area, while charming and modest, is not cheap, but it does promise splendid living. There's salmon fishing, early-morning swims in Howe Sound (never crowded and dog-friendly), a charming library, many literary gatherings and, from what I heard, a ton of extreme outdoor activities for the older types. One friend's mother is about to take an excursion to Canada's far northern province, a trip he and others call a "geri-Arctic" vacation.

And if you're so inclined, there's "premium marijuana delivered to your door in 60 minutes." That's according to the flyer at the corner of Granville and Georgia streets in downtown Vancouver. It was taped to the utility pole near the bus stop where, with dozens of other people, I lined up (politely, of course: this is Canada, where the joke goes that if you happen to step on someone's foot in an elevator, the other person is apt to apologize). We were all waiting to catch the 257 express to Horseshoe Bay. The sign and pole sit right outside the stately Hudson's Bay Company, a six-story building (or "storey," if you're a Canadian, the same as the word "process" is pronounced with a long "o"). Hudson's Bay is a stunning 1927 terra cotta building with Corinthian columns.

"Hey, it's Canada," said the Chilean cousin, who used to live in B.C., of the specialized delivery service. She said the same thing when I hesitated going into the water because it was so much colder than I'm used to.

"Hey, it's Canada."

Except the days I spent there were seeing record warm temperatures. Too hot to hike, my cousin said. So we stayed indoors. We talked books, talked plants, watched her daughter cook vegan corn fritters (using garbanzo flour and chia seeds instead of eggs), grilled shrimp from Argentina, salmon from down the road.

We had plenty to talk about, if we chose to. Who else knew or knows better our respective mothers and fathers—all long gone—and the complicated relationships with siblings? Who else could claim the same grandparents, who shared the same Sunday morning lox-and-bagel brunches at the grandparents' house in Huntington Woods, Michigan? We did a bit of that, reviewing where Nana kept the candy, how she made her chopped liver, what everyone made for Thanksgiving, what we did in those decades when we didn't see one another. There was plenty of sensitive and unanswered material to nurse and rehearse (and we've done it in the past). Instead we settled down in her bedroom with strong coffee and a bowl of almonds to watch tennis on TV from the Rogers Cup in Toronto. After her husband grew ill, my cousin, never an athlete, more an artist, grew quite fond of watching the sport. It distracted her, she said. At this point, she knows more of the players than I do and I've been following it a long time.

She had taped the match, so we could have fast-forwarded to see the results. We didn't. We suffered through the misses and winners of the young Stefanos Tsitsipas, a darling 19-year-old Greek we favored, in his match with the square-looking, thirtysomething Kevin Anderson from South Africa, whooping and hollering all the way to the end when the Greek hit the lines, when he won the match, a day before turning 20.

We're going to remember that match. We're going to remember that day in her bedroom. Nothing precious, nothing sentimental. Just time together.

The next morning when I headed for the ferry, she packed me some leftover tzatziki, a little salmon, a piece of flourless chocolate cake and a cloth napkin.

"I knew you'd like a cloth napkin, cuz," she said. "I know you." She was right about that. I love cloth napkins. I love her.

8/18/18

"Dear Jane,

Awhile ago I took some of you garden sculptures. They were a great start for my junk garden, but I know how valuable they can become. So I return them with my apologies. Thanks for the rust!

—YOUR FELLOW GARDENER

SAVANNAH

1 / *An Orange hat and a Black church (Speak their name)*

It's a little scary going to a strange place, especially if it's to a Black church. That's when it's good to wear an orange hat.

"I sure do like that hat," said a woman on Montgomery Street after I got out of my car. "Can I have it?"

I could tell she meant it.

"I have way too much stuff," I answered. "So I would love to give it to you, but I love my hat, too."

She busted out laughing (don't you love "busted out" instead of "burst out"?) and grabbed me in a hug, not an air hug but a real one, real close. That's how they do at First African Baptist Church.

"Where are you from?" another woman holding a pencil and piece of paper asked as soon as I walked up the stairs to the crowded front parlor of the red brick building on Franklin Square, a church that used to be called First Colored Baptist. The pews, which were made by enslaved people, are nailed into the floor. Beneath the auditorium floor is a sub-floor known as the Underground Railroad floor. That's where runaway slaves would hide as they made their way north. The air holes, as necessary for life as was their perilous journey, were drilled into the wood. They still exist.

Next to me, also waiting to go into the sanctuary, a couple said, "Ontario, Canada." Another said, "Chesterfield, Virginia." Still another, "Richmond, Virginia."

I finally said, "Fiftieth Street, Savannah, Georgia."

The church was nearly filled when I walked in. I was meeting a friend from Vancouver, Canada, who had done her research before visiting. This was her first trip to Savannah and this was the historic Black church she wanted to visit. Rev. Thurmond Tillman was away on family business in Florida that week, so Rev. Paul Little took over. Many women were wearing hats. Rev. Little started off by asking people in the congregation to report how so-and-so was doing. They shouted their responses: "In the hospital," "out of the hospital," "in for procedures," "out for tests." Then he asked again: "Who are you praying for? Speak their name." Then he implored, "Someone shout out, 'I'm covered'." More than one replied, "I'm covered!" He called for anyone who was praying for someone to come forth. We held back, Mary Burns from Vancouver and I from 50th Street. But who doesn't have someone they're praying for? It didn't take long to lose our inhibition. We walked up and joined most of the congregation who had moved forward. We held hands. We hugged. Our eyes grew full. It was healing.

Without knowing it, I came for some of that healing. I came for succor. Yes, digging in the garden is good for the soul. Yes, standing shoulder to shoulder at an oyster roast on the edge of the continent on a beautiful if blustery day is healing, especially after the sun, absent for what seemed forever, finally showed itself. Yes, going to a fundraiser on a Saturday afternoon for a brave woman with lung cancer who is having trouble paying the bills helps to soften the pain. But it's not everything.

For no particular reason I was aware of, I returned a few months later to that church. I returned alone. Wearing the same orange hat, I walked in shoulder to shoulder with some people I recognized from my last visit and a bunch of new people I did not know.

Before the readings or the words, Rev. Tillman said it was time for fellowship. Not just with the person next to you or in front or behind you. To the faint sound of a bass guitar, an organ, a tambourine and just the hint of a drumbeat, we got up and walked around and hugged and shook hands. The men did that shoulder-banging greeting thing. The women, not to be too gender specific, hugged, really hugged.

A group of kids, wearing white shirts (their ties flying) and pressed pants, bounded to the front, passed around the microphone and read the words of Martin Luther King, Jr. "Free at last, free at last." The congregation, some standing, arms waving, fingers pointing, shoulders swaying, heads shaking, cheered them on.

And then Rev. Tillman asked the hard questions.

"Why would Martin Luther King, Jr. put it all on the line?" he asked, his lanky body moving backward then forward. "He had it made. Why not just let things be the way they were?

"Dr. King never said he hated white people," Tillman said, pausing. "He spoke only love."

After that, the good reverend recognized a "young brother" who was celebrating ten years of sobriety, a Miss Black USA and a former Miss Black USA. He gave the details of someone who would be "funeralized today."

Two hours later, I walked out, still in my orange hat, full and fulfilled. It's good to take time in fellowship, even if it's in a strange place with people you don't know.

1/25/15

2 / Bless your heart
(Sarcastic? Nah)

For some ridiculous reason that fall day in September, we decided to take the car when meeting people at Olympia Cafe, still one of the best restaurants in a fleet of newcomers in this newly popular city. Oh, we'll find parking, we said or thought. How hard can it be? Well, very hard.

Has anyone been to River Street lately? Can you say *half the universe?* OK, it was Saturday night, Labor Day weekend and First Saturday on the river. Still. We could have taken a cab. We could have called an Uber. No. We drove, only to find all the parking lots full. All of them. Old habits. Hard to break.

"Where's Tom?" someone asked when we walked in, since we left the house with him.

"He's parking," I said of our driver, someone who that day had already driven in from Atlanta. "I expect we'll see him sometime next month. Bless his heart."

A few days later, I ran into someone I know, "sort of." We both were in the Andrew Carnegie library on Bull Street, standing in line to check out a book.

To "sort of" know someone could mean we know someone in common. It might be someone introduced to us—once. It might be someone with whom we shared a regular activity—like the mornings we'd meet to swim at the Aquatic Center—without really saying more than three words, which was the case in the library.

"You still swimming?" he asked while fingering a book.

"Not really," I said. "Certainly not at 4:30 a.m."

"Craig's still swimming," he said, mentioning someone we both knew, who swam in a nearby lane.

"Bless his heart," I said, remembering driving in the dark to practice (no traffic), taking that initial dive into the pool (always cold), never making it out of the slow lane (the party lane).

Those three words—"bless his heart"—were starting to be a theme, maybe even a meme, although I'm still not sure I know what "meme" means. If so, it beats "No worries" or "Enjoy your day," my two least favorite phrases, followed by "It's all good" (especially when it's not) or "Are you still working on that?" referencing something I'm eating, which is never, in my mind, something I have to work at.

I used to think "bless her heart" was pejorative, a bit on the sarcastic side, maybe a little passive-aggressive ("She still thinks she can wear that dress, bless her heart"). That was before I moved into my third decade of living in the South. (For the record, I don't know anyone up North who uses that phrase or who would know how to respond to it.)

Now I use it all the time. "Bless your heart," I say to our 18-year-old cat, Mama Mia, who slinks to the bowl on the front porch, maneuvering her long, multi-segmented body like a low-riding Oldsmobile from the outside nest of leaves and debris she's made for herself, as she chews each piece of dry food, slowly, carefully, deliberately.
That could be a sympathetic use of the phrase.

It doesn't always turn out that way. When I hear myself saying "bless their hearts" as I read what's supposed to be one hundred seeds in a packet of collard greens when it looks to be closer to fifty (but who wants to stop and count each one of those?), I think of the seed company, but instead of counting or complaining, I say, "Bless their hearts."

And then I hear myself offer it up to Sandy West, Ossabaw Island's sporty and amazing doyenne, then 105, as she spots one of her favorite men, a beloved doctor. She was eating dinner in a crowded dining room. "Hubba, hubba, there goes Bubba," she says before anyone else recognizes him, putting down her fork long enough to pat her chest and pretend to swoon.

"Bless her heart," I say for the tenth time that day—for Sandy's ability to spot Dr. Bubba before anyone else did, for responding to him, for coming up with the rhyme to match the name with the expression, for being 105 years..

She's a pretty good eater, too, bless her heart.

9/8/18

3 / *And you are from where?*
(But what's your sign?)

"So where are you from?"

Now there's a loaded question if I ever heard one. It doesn't stop us from asking. All the time. Anytime we meet someone new. It seems important to know, as if it will tell us something about the person. But does it? Think of all the people you know from the same city, even the same block—dare we say the same family?—as yourself. Does living in the same city make you and/or your sibs or the elementary school friends down the block at all alike? I doubt it.

So why do we want to know where someone is from? Yes, there are Midwestern values, but there are also Northwest values and Southern values. Besides, it's such a mobile population it doesn't matter anymore. Maybe it's just a conversation filler, but it's beginning to sound like another question we hardly hear anymore, although at one time it ranked right up there with wanting to know where we are from: "What's your sign?"

At one point that was important, too, until we realized there are only twelve astrological signs (I know, there are the moons, the planets and the elements to consider, too) and the possibilities of sharing characteristics, meaningful characteristics, with one-twelfth of the world is rather foolish, although it's always fun to find someone who shares your birthday. A Taurus! I knew it! Why didn't you say you were a Scorpio? Now I understand.

Forget astrology. Today we Google people to find out all the relevant—or irrelevant—things we used to find out by reading their chart, except now we're beginning to realize (or remember) the best way to get to know someone is to talk to them, face to face, and leave the rest to fiction. (Do I really need to check in on Facebook or Brad Pitt or Lily Tomlin every day?)

"So where are you from?" someone asked me the other day.

"The Midwest," I said, thinking that covered it pretty well. To say Michigan is too broad. Michigan is a big, big state. Saying you're a Yooper (that means you're from the Upper Peninsula) has nothing to do with Saginaw or Grand Rapids.

To say I'm from Detroit is misleading since I'm from a suburb of Detroit. Saying I'm from Huntington Woods, which is a bus ride down Woodward Avenue to downtown Detroit, doesn't mean anything to anyone unless they're from nearby suburbs like Royal Oak or Ferndale or Oak Park. It tells you where my parents—may they rest in peace— lived when they were starting a family. They chose the suburb. I did not. Later, I would move away. As my mother, visiting me in Chicago (or somewhere else), once said to me about something or other: "I did not raise you to be this way." She was not angry. She was just stating a fact.

Children become their own people. They carve out their own lives no matter their astrological signs, no matter their birthplace, no matter their parents.

"The Midwest?" the man repeated when I said where I was from. "You mean Phoenix?"

He may be good at what he does, but that would not include geography.

"So where are you from?"

What does that mean? Are you asking where did I live before I moved to Savannah? To me, that begs the more interesting, more relevant question: Why did you move to Savannah?

Maybe the most noteworthy question is "Where were you born?"—especially if you wanted to know something about a person's roots. So are other questions: "Did your parents get divorced? Did they fight much? What kind of relationship did you have with your siblings?" Except we don't ask these questions.

I was reared in Michigan with my designated nuclear unit and the blessed spring-blooming forsythia, lilacs and peonies and the sunny days of winter, of lost mittens, of snowball fights, of walks in the blindingly bright snow with wet feet. If that sounds like a long time ago, it's because it was.

But I "grew up" in Chicago. That's where, on my own after college, I entered the real world of rent, strangers, parking tickets, work, bosses, disappointments, high-rise buildings, economic disparity and the angst of stumbling through my twenties. There was plenty of confusion, commotion, agitation, gray days, gray skies, gray moods and cold weather.

During one of our "cold" spells last week—and because I am from Michigan—I got this statement a lot: "You must love this cold weather," like people would know.

Wrong. I hate cold weather. If I loved cold weather, I would be living in a place with cold weather.

This is where I live. Right now, this is where I am from. Savannah, Georgia.

1/26/19

4 / Stepping up and into Brighter Day (Best case scenario)

All things considered, it's great news. But that's not your first thought. Not by a long shot. It's kind of like when someone you've worked with for years, someone who knows what you like in your coffee, who doesn't mind covering for you when you have to do some important business, who brings you peanut butter sandwiches because you don't trust yourself to keep peanut butter in the house, tells you they got a dream job. But they have to leave town. "Isn't that great?" they say.

Or when a neighbor—who has the keys to your house and is familiar with feeding your chickens and likes walking your dogs—breaks the news: "I'm getting married and moving to Portland, Oregon."

How about when a postal carrier you've known for years, who goes the extra mile to get you that package and knows how to open your ornery screen door, gets reassigned to something closer to their home, explaining, "It cuts hours off my drive time."

Or, worse yet, when your dentist retires, just after you've broken him or her into your acceptable pain level and laughs at your jokes, who, truth be told, looks so relaxed when you see him out in the world you barely recognize him, says, "Isn't that terrific?"

None of those announcements is the end of the world. Each time, you act excited and say how happy you are for them—even if inside you are thinking, "What?! You're doing what? Really? What about me? Have you thought how that will affect *my* life? No."

Me-me-me.

That's when you take a step back, away from the tsunami of the moment, and draw a deep breath. That's when you realize the sale of Brighter Day Natural Foods Market from longtime (and original) owners, Peter and Janie Brodhead, to Kristin Russell and Brad Baugh is as good as it could get.

Frankly, folks, it couldn't have been better.

The Brodheads are leaving at the top of their game. Kristin and Brad, longtime neighbors and customers (sometimes daily) of the store, are filling the gap to keep the independent and eclectic center for all that's healthy and good on the corner of Park Avenue and Bull Street.

Both 65, Janie and Peter could have retired—or "refired," as Janie says. They've been at this retail business for forty-one years. It's been their passion. By now, they could have given it up and no one would have blamed them. But that didn't feel right. Enter Kristin and Brad, in their mid-40s, believers in herbal medicine, devotees of healthy living.

After the first ten years, Janie and Peter could have passed along to employees the most inglorious or mundane of tasks required in running a business. But there was Janie, bending, kneeling, schlepping, filling shelves, straightening products so their labels faced front, spotting holes where the last bottle or the last bag had been sold, taking over the register when someone left to find a price, doing inventory—all the while maintaining eye contact, asking about the grandkids, flirting with a baby, inquiring after your bum knee, offering solace to constant sneezing ("It's the season"), wondering how you're going to cook that burdock.

There was Peter, three or four people waiting to talk to him about how to use a first aid ointment, the best way to ingest some homeopathic pills or where to find an esoteric vitamin, patiently flipping through his books, resorting to the computer, printing out a protocol for fighting a lingering cold, giving his full attention to whomever he was talking to, with humor, sincerity, optimism and decades of cultivated knowledge.

Next door, there was Kristin at the Sentient Bean, a coffeehouse she and a partner started in 2001, clearing tables, washing dishes when she had to, taking orders at the counter, filling coffee bins, the steady hand (and brains) behind the eminently successful Forsyth Farmers' Market, a project she and four others initiated some ten years ago. You'd think one of them—Kristin, Brad or the Brodheads—would have felt threatened by the Market, which in many cases included vendors offering the same things their businesses sold. Coffee, carrots, bread, sandwiches, broccoli, pasta, sweet rolls, nuts, collards, lettuce. That is the capitalist model, after all. They didn't. You'd think the Brodheads could have been threatened by Kristin's business. They weren't. Each party chose cooperation over competition, respect over disdain.

I will miss Janie and Peter. They carry important institutional memory. Just recently, Janie said one of their first customers in 1978 was Sandy West, the doyen of Ossabaw Island. Sandy's about to turn 107.

I applaud Kristin and Brad for seeing a need and stepping up. Win-win.

12/1/19

5 / Neighbors
(Kismet or something
like that)

Today I met Jellybean, Elizabeth and Chester. They're neighbors.

Did you just move in? I ask.

About a year ago.

How did I not know this? There's just so much to remember.

That same day, I heard a gentle knock on my front door from a young girl with a sweet, familiar face. I've seen that face before, I think. I know that face. But where? Who is it? She's so tall. I stall, waiting for memory to catch up to what's in front of me.

She plunges right in without giving me a single clue.

Can I get a ride with you to the plant swap?

Of course, I answer, so happy someone would ask. And then the coin drops. I know her. But not before I see the 10-year-old, the 7-year-old, the 5-year-old versions of her. They change so much. Who does she see when she looks at me?

Oh, to hold back, to refrain from saying: I went to your third birthday party. (Or, something I could have said to someone else: I went to your bris).

People come. People go. Memories linger.

This week there's a PODS (Portable On Demand Storage) unit on my street. A neighbor is moving away. Today, she returned the key to our house, the one we gave her in case we needed her for dog-walking or chicken-feeding duty. The transfer made me sort of sad. It's comforting to know someone else has your key and your back. "Don't you want to keep it a little longer?" I think to myself.

Some part of me wants to curl up in that PODS unit and move across the country, too. How liberating to be in a new city with new weather patterns, new skies, new smells in the air, new people to meet, new nooks and crannies to explore. How nice to be a newcomer, when you don't know where any of the bones are buried, you don't know so-and-so's first wife or a neighbor's second husband, you don't know someone even had a first wife, let alone a second.

How freeing not to know who used to live in what house and how the gardens used to be tended "back when people cared."

How exciting to drive down a street where nobody knows your car, where you aren't comparing this city manager to an earlier city manager, where you don't pass a corner/a house/a street and remember a certain homicide from a certain year.

Where you don't know nothing 'bout no one.

How nice to be forced to divest yourself of "things"—flower vases, cutlery, bowls, CDs, pillows, blankets, standing lamps, lampshades, tablecloths. I just cleaned out a crawl space and found two boomboxes, two vacuum cleaners, three old-fashioned hard suitcases, a black-and-white TV my Aunt Trudy gave me when I went to college, notebooks, a three-ton Webster's dictionary, cords, plugs, chargers.

On the other hand, how could I get someone in a new city to help me move a heavy dresser if I didn't know anyone in town? How could I say to a new neighbor: "I need someone strong for 30 minutes and I need him (or her) right now" (as I did to a trusty old neighbor) and then to hear in reply, "I'll call my boyfriend; he's retired." And then to have said boyfriend show up.

Earlier this week, I tried to make a reservation online to a new restaurant in town. I didn't want to do it that way. I know it costs the restaurant a buck every time someone does that, but it was just so easy and I needed to do it while I was thinking of it.

"La Scala," I type, followed by the date and the time. Bingo. I have reservations for next week. As long as arancini (stuffed rice balls)—served at a glorious, surreal soft opening a few weeks ago—are on the menu, I'll be happy.

But wait! There's something else, something strange. The

restaurant—or so I read—that sits in the beautiful turn-of-the-century house at the corner of Abercorn and 37th streets with all the stained glass and those beautiful grounds and a top floor that used to be a convent, is in a "historic Italian neighborhood." That's what it said. I laughed.

With one Italian restaurant, albeit a beautiful one, Savannah now has an Italian neighborhood? How did I not know this? I look again. It turns out this Italian neighborhood is in Baltimore, not Savannah. We have many things in common, Baltimore and Savannah. Crab cakes. A waterfront. History. And now a restaurant named La Scala. But only one city has as an Italian neighborhood.

And only one La Scala shares a block with another Savannah great, Elizabeth on 37th.

As it would happen—maybe it's kismet, maybe it's the size of the town—Jeffrey Downey and Donald Lubowicki, the affable, hard-working geniuses behind La Scala (and Circa 1875 on Whitaker Street) worked at Elizabeth when they first got to town.

"I wish them well," said Greg Butch, who, with his brother Gary, now owns Elizabeth on 37th. "I've known them forever. They're great. We're all friends."

Now that's what I call neighborly.

10/13/18

6 / *Looking for watermelons (Not so easy)*

On that early morning in July when we were looking for watermelons, no one showed up with "a wagon and a horse in the summer sun." That's a lyric from the underrated and basically unknown songwriter extraordinaire Oscar Brown Jr. in his classic rendition of the song "Watermelon Man" on his iconic 1960 album "Sin & Soul...and Then Some."

We did not have Herbie Hancock's piano version—or Cuban percussionist Mongo Santamaría's—playing in our heads. We sure enough did not run into any watermelon tagged "organic." But by golly, by the end of the day—and it was a long day—we nailed our assignment.

Last week, Promised Land Farm's Robert Johnson and I showed up with watermelon aplenty for Deep Center's East Side Block Party because that's what block party organizer phenom Keith Miller wanted—local watermelon (not what you buy at the grocery store but melons straight outta the field)—to serve to all the young poets after they rapped and rhymed their down-and-dirty, heartfelt truths about life on the street in 2017 to family and friends and folks like former Mayor Otis Johnson and Juvenile Court Judge LeRoy Burke III at East Broad Elementary.

"They're huge," Miller said of the watermelons in the haul. "I was expecting those little round ones."

No siree, Bob. We came back with the real deal. Crimson sweet, thank you very much.

It took some hunting, driving around in Robert's nephew's truck (not Robert's 1952 'Mater Mobile). We tried Clyde's Market in Pembroke, the Black Creek Feed & Seed in Ellabell, Hodges Strawberry Farm in Newington, Ken's IGA in Ellabell, taking the back roads all the way.

"My wife sings in a church down that dirt road," Robert said. "This here is where I grew up. That's where I picked cotton. You do not want to pick cotton. Hard, hard work."

There's always Kroger, someone texted me. I was tempted. Nope, said Robert. Give me half a minute. We gonna find us some watermelon, he said. We kept on, windows open (swatting gnats), windows closed (too many gnats).

We were hunting a watermelon patch. We wanted a u-pick-'em field. Somewhere in these South Georgia fields we were going to find the source, the mother lode, the beginning. But we were getting discouraged. We stopped at a farm stand in Brooklet (pop. 1,113) in Bulloch County, three hundred sixty-four people per square mile, median income $34,438, home of the annual Brooklet Peanut Festival. Not too far from a town called Denmark.

This is our last stop, said I, the impatient one. The woman tending the stand had a lead for us. She got on her phone, punched in the numbers, called her source and gave us directions to Lloyd and Deanna Strickland's farm on Highway 67. A couple of rights, a left, another right at the old tractor across from the two-story blue house, then down a shake-and-bake road.

Bingo! Watermelons. And corn. And canary melons. And peas. And gnats, no extra charge.

We weren't the only ones standing in the shade by our vehicles waiting for a crew to drive in from the fields with a fresh batch. This time we were patient. Finally, after some fancy negotiating in broken Spanish with people who know more English than I know Spanish, we got back in the truck and followed a crew of six down paths through the field. We stopped. The farm workers jumped off the back of the truck, dispersed, squatted down to cut the vines, stood up, formed a line and started tossing the thirty-five- to forty-pound melons (they might as well have been medicine balls) to the crew chief in the back of the truck.

This is not easy work. This is what you call migrant labor. This is why—or so I read—any crackdown on immigrants, which is supposed to help U.S. citizens, is managing to create a labor shortage in California. This despite a raise in pay to $16 an hour, health insurance benefits and paid vacations. And that's in California. No one wants to do this work. P.S.: It's not hard to see why. It's hot, it's gnatty, it's brutal, it's constant. I'm glad I wasn't out there snipping vines, hoisting the melons and passing them down the human chain.

Along the way, the crew chief deliberately dropped a somewhat damaged melon for us gringos to try. Splat. Smoosh. Grab. "Go for the middle," he said. "It's the sweetest." No kidding.

Back in town, we transferred the melons to my truck. Then I crammed the truck for safekeeping into a neighbor's garage overnight, squeezing past lawn mowers, bikes, boxes. The next day I drove my haul to East Broad Elementary where Keith, the good-humored Energizer Bunny, had a citified crew from Dare Dukes' Deep Center waiting for me to make the final transfer.

They didn't complain too much, if at all, but I wish they could have been with me the day before. I wish the students—the young poets—could have put their poetic eyes and imaginative words on farm work. As articulate as they were about urban ills, urban challenges, social justice, I'd like to see what they would say about spending a day in the fields. None of it is easy.

7/9/19

7 / Summer in Savannah: Waiting for field peas, eating figs (Worth the wait)

And they say, kids grow up fast. You look away for a minute; the next time you see them, they're walking, they're talking, they're winking, whistling, turning cartwheels, cracking up at their own jokes, riding a skateboard, flapping their arms and saying, "I feel so free." They're tying their own shoelaces, enforcing social distancing during the pandemic with a six-foot stick, explaining (patiently, no judgment) over the phone on Messenger Kids how to get your volume turned up, how to turn the image right side up.

Then there are field peas. You plant them, one little dried pea at a time, wondering all along how this desiccated, unattractive bit of DNA will turn into anything worthwhile. You're not quite sure they'll grow. It's your first time planting them because, well, who doesn't have extra time at home during these pandemic days to try something new? Anyway, you're not from here. People up North plant tomatoes. They don't plant field peas. Some of my smartest friends don't even know what field peas are. They may eat black-eyed peas on New Year's Day but that's about it.

Sometime in June—maybe May, who can keep track?—you push them into the ground, not quite sure how much space they'll need. They're Whippoorwill Southern peas, also known as cowpeas, and they go back a long way. Enslaved people brought them to the Americas from Africa, according to Southern Exposure Seed Exchange, tucked away in pockets or satchels or in their braided hair. They were that precious. What hardy peas, not unlike their owners. They're survivors. They had to be after those brutal transatlantic crossings. Thomas Jefferson grew Whippoorwills at Monticello, where hundreds (hundreds!) of enslaved folks worked his famous gardens.

You plant them, then you forget about them. You read a book. Or two. You start watching "Trumbo" with Bryan Cranston about the House on Un-American Activities Committee and you think the more things change, the more they stay the same. You watch your eggplant flower, your yard-long Chinese beans lengthen, your bush beans produce and your zinnias (the official flower of Tybee Island) grow taller.

You turn your back on the field peas. Being a bit superstitious, you try not to expect too much until the day you look closer and see the vines are wrapping around one another, climbing up and through the (barren) lime tree, crawling over the basil, scaling the palm tree, covering up the Padrón peppers, affixing to the nearby concrete wall. Overnight, they seem to have sneaked through the discarded tomato cages you've wired together with soft twisty ties, Howard Finster-style.

With nothing else to pick, you turn your attention to the okra— knowing all the while if you don't get those suckers the minute they start to grow, they will be woody and inedible. Then, with all those seeds rattling inside, they will be worth more as acoustic instruments than as food. What a wonderful four-letter word: okra, yet another product of Africa, another member of the mallow family, a kissing cousin to hibiscus and cotton, all with those showy, magnificent blooms.

But still no peas. Nothing to do now but pick figs. Talk about a short growing season. Talk about something that grows up overnight. I have a friend on Tybee who has staked out five or six productive trees. This is the week she starts riding her bicycle past said trees. Her reasoning is sound. You have to pick those figs quickly, as in now. Their "shelf life" is about a minute; they spoil easily. That is, if the birds don't get there first because they are watching, too. They are circling around waiting for the appropriate time to strike. They eat them raw. We do, too, if we don't bake, roast, grill, stuff or caramelize them, or blend them into smoothies or dip them in chocolate.

Peas, I learn, love hot, hot weather, the kind we are finally getting.

Field peas seem to plump out overnight. That's when you can start picking and shelling, either on the front porch or while you watch the end of "Trumbo." It's work. They don't pop out like sugar snap peas. The bunch I picked this week—with both hands circling the stash—yielded a cup of peas. Not much. Forget refrigerating, freezing or postponing. I heated up the skillet and tossed those puppies into a pan of sizzling sautéed garlic the same day I heard from someone vacationing in Maine. She was so cold she had to put on wool socks. No fresh figs—or field peas—for her.

7/19/20

8 / *Waiting for Hurricane Matthew and canoeing the Ebenezer (The quiet of the river)*

Yes, last week's storm, nature's version of a major tree-trimming event, was a mess. We still have debris on the curb.

Yes, it was a bit of a crapshoot: who would lose a roof, a car window, maybe a chimney? Who would lose power? Some houses on our street were lit up, others stood dark.

Yes, it was inconvenient to be without power for up to thirty-six hours. No AC, no window fans, no microwave, no electric toothbrush, no clock (the kind with minute hands), no Magic Bullet, no washing machine, no charging capacity (unless you got in your car and took a drive, carbon footprint be damned, assuming you had a car with that feature).

Yes, it was hot, especially when the high winds died down and the drama had passed, especially in the middle of the night when it was so hot you had to practically will yourself to sleep.

But in the end it was quiet—hushed, you might say—and that's what I'll remember and appreciate the most. The refrigerator that constantly cuts on and off and drives you (me) crazy? Silenced. The outdoor heating and cooling return so inconveniently situated that it interrupts, intrudes and infringes on conversation? Muzzled.

In the end, it was a good excuse to rid your fridge of leftovers and condiments that had turned blue, limes as hard as golf balls and mystery food from the freezer; a great excuse to sit on your front stoop with morning coffee and talk to your neighbors, because no one wants to stay inside a stuffy house; and it was a good reminder of how pleasant it is to sit around a table and eat dinner by candlelight, the more candles the better. Maybe we can remember these things and do them more often.

In the end, the only thing quieter than going about your day without electricity, without stressing about all the defrosted food (some you want, some you don't), without worrying about when exactly the power would return, without fretting about where you fit into the electric grid—the only thing quieter is to be canoeing on Ebenezer Creek, to be navigating under your own steam.

It doesn't start out that way, especially if you don't know your canoeing partner.

"Uh, boat-mate," you may venture, because if you're canoeing with someone you just met, as I was, and you don't remember names very well, as I don't, and she, not a great swimmer, was more concerned about falling in the dark water and endangering her expensive hearing aids than following your instructions, the start of the paddle can be a bit rocky. "Pick a side. Any side," I say, trying to be diplomatic. "Then stick with it."

But after a while, in between chinwags (because what better place to have a good old-fashioned exchange than in a canoe on Ebenezer Creek, where the only sound is that of a pileated woodpecker or the screech of a red-shouldered hawk catching a thermal) you begin to find a rhythm, which earns you the name "Stern Master."

All because sometime a million years ago at overnight camp you learned the J-Stroke.

Aside from learning a diplomatic way to talk to your partner in the boat, the J-Stroke is about all you need to know in canoeing. That alone makes you seem like an expert. I'm not sure what it has to do with the letter J. It's really just a way to steer the boat so you don't run into some of the overhanging limbs that might—just might—be carrying a water moccasin. It's a way to steer the boat over to the towering tupelo trees or the flared trunks of the powerful cypress knees (which look more like billowing skirts), some of which are over a thousand years old, so you can fish a Styrofoam cup out of the water or so you can get a better view of the greenish legs of a little blue heron.

The water, black from the tannin of decaying leaves, was calm. The level, which seemed fine to me, is determined by the U.S. Army Corps of Engineers, which decides when the floodgates to the Savannah River should be opened. I'm thinking the best time to canoe would be when the water is released.

We paddled on a Saturday, the day after the storm. If I expected crowds, I was wrong. Maybe everyone was at home cleaning up after the storm. If I expected debris, I was wrong again. There was very little litter to pick up. On one hand, I was grateful the creek, a tributary of the Savannah River, was so quiet and that it was so easy to get in and get out. On the other hand, I wonder: Why don't more people go out there? If you value quiet, if you want to get away from the screen, if you want to feel your shoulders drop a few inches, Ebenezer Creek is the place to be. Just don't tell too many people.

9/15/16

9 / Namaste here/ Hurricane Dorian (Another look at curfew)

If you've ever wondered what Savannah was like twenty-five years ago—before hotels tried to take over residential neighborhoods (can you say the "boutique" hotel going up at Tattnall and Liberty streets?), before an art school grew to more than fifteen thousand students without requiring the school to provide parking lots (can you remember finding parking downtown?), before said art school began snatching up large properties (and not paying property taxes because it's a nonprofit), before more city money was directed to the beautification of downtown squares than to cleaning out neighborhood storm drains to alleviate flooding, before large crews of landscape workers began popping up to blow leaves and grass into the storm drains, before corporate America began its destructive march to destroy small businesses (can you say Home Depot vs. Thrifty Hardware?), before the current "if it bleeds, it leads" mentality in the delivery of news, and the fear-baiting notices on social media made people suspicious if a stranger walked down their street and looked a little too long at a car—then maybe this past week will give you a clue.

Despite the early media lead-up to Hurricane Dorian and the destruction to The Bahamas, the whole thing was kinda nice, starting with a crowded and warm reception for Panhandle Slim when Sulphur Studios held a one-night-only show of his original, quirky work. That was the night a seven-year-old named Oz, a miniature version of Scott Stanton (Mr. Slim), sat out front on a stool and played his guitar, his guitar case open for donations, busking for coins; when people who live south of DeRenne Avenue ventured into town because they needed to see for themselves just who this Panhandle Slim is.

For those of us who decided not to evacuate, we had the town to ourselves. Some of us had a good chuckle at the word "curfew," remembering earlier times when "curfew" meant disobeying the rules, when it meant sneaking into dorm rooms past "curfew."

With higher-than-usual winds and 24/7 hurricane prognostications, we got to hear from worried out-of-town friends just figuring out Savannah resides on the coast (and the edge of the continent).

We got to clear out our fridge in anticipation of downed electrical lines (and in the process see open shelves and a blinding light in the back of the shelves). We had a good excuse to clean drawers as we looked for batteries (so many pens, so many dead batteries, all those Christmas cards from 10 years ago). We took the time to paw through the detritus under the sink in search of pitchers for water (finding dozens of old sponges, new sponges, half-used bottles of dish detergent). We had the time to figure out how to activate subtitles on our TV/ movie devices, so we could watch foreign films and better hear British dramas.

Thank you, neighbors who communicated that they would or would not be leaving. Thank you, Grey Market for bucking the trend and staying open. Thank you, Margaret and the rest of the folks at AutoZone for answering last-minute car concerns—and helping me find the dipstick under the hood of my car.

Imagine going into The Book Lady on Liberty Street to pick up something new to read in anticipation of Hurricane Dorian and finding the aisles of that one-of-a-kind bookstore crowded. "Evacuees from Florida," deadpanned Chris from behind the front desk. The good news is I picked up a copy of Oscar Wilde's *The Picture of Dorian Gray*, the name on everyone's mind, and thinking for maybe the tenth time I should read it, before perusing a few sentences and putting it back on the shelf. Maybe I don't have to read this. Ever. Maybe I'll just watch the movie instead, the 1945 classic with Peter Lawford, Donna Reed, George Sanders and Angela Lansbury. Or maybe not.

Imagine seeing a crush of people in Brighter Day Natural Foods

Market, all with the same reaction. "I didn't know there still were places like this," said one evacuee from Florida.

We can't go back to those years before Savannah was "discovered." We don't want to. They were fraught, like most times. We can't change what has happened, but it was a nice reminder of the small town we once were. It was nice to know we have one another's backs.

Y'all leaving?

Namaste here. (Translation: Nah, I'm going to stay).

Namaste.

9/8/19

10 / *I love you, Savannah,*
I don't always like you
(Like lovers quarreling)

It was an honest enough discussion about Savannah, where I've lived for thirty years. On one side of the equation? New friends. Newcomers to Savannah. Honeymooners. They can't get enough of this crazy coastal town. They can't stop smiling. They can't stop grinning. Their sense of satisfaction stretches all the way up the Eastern seacoast, from Boston, which they vacated after retiring, to Savannah, which they adopted some four years ago. They're part-timers, for the moment.

They're smitten. They know every square. They've been to every neighborhood association event and celebration. They march in the squares, take classes at the senior center (where they'll eventually teach a class on film), craft cornhole boards at Maven Makers on West Boundary Street, go to the new jazz club on Broughton Street. They love Rancho Alegre Cuban Restaurant.

They're frequent visitors to the Ralph Mark Gilbert Civil Rights Museum on Martin Luther King Jr., Blvd. They've taken many tours of Congregation Mickve Israel. They're well-versed on Savannah's shameful history regarding slavery. They've been to Macon. In a few weeks they're off to the Okefenokee Swamp. They love the downtown Kroger, First African Baptist Church and the Tybee Post Theater, in no particular order. They've made friends through Drinking Liberally Savannah, a political group that meets regularly. They went to SCAD's Savannah Women of Vision ceremony without knowing anyone being celebrated.

Unlike some newcomers or visitors, they don't rely on me for directions, suggestions or ideas of things to do (although I did arrange for a great boat ride through the marsh, around the Tybee coast). They read the calendars of things to do in the newspaper. They take advantage of The Learning Center at Senior Citizens, Inc.

I'm delighted they're here. They're smart. They're funny. We have a few friends in common from Detroit, which is nice. They've been around the block a few times. We share some of the same Midwestern values.

But mostly I keep my opinions—about Savannah—to myself. Who wants to be a party pooper or a killjoy? I remember the honeymoon period. One of the first people I met and liked when I started as a reporter for the Savannah Morning News was a woman who was on her way out when I was on my way in. She was leaving the paper—and eventually Savannah—months after I moved here. Knowing how susceptible I am to opinions from people I like, people who speak truth, I knew I couldn't be her friend. Just yet. I had to keep my distance. I was in my own honeymoon period. I loved my job. I loved Savannah. I didn't want to know too much, be too critical. I didn't want anything or anyone raining on my parade.

I understand the enthusiasm of my Boston friends. I also understand the folly of saying, "But you should have seen it then!" But jeez Louise, can we talk?

It's one thing not to like change. We as human beings want things to stay the same. We gripe when Back in the Day Bakery changes its hours. We moan about the demise of free parking on Broughton Street and the new hours—8 until 8, six days a week. We weep and wail about construction of yet another hotel. We don't understand bad architecture. We really don't understand the proposed extra tax from the fire department. We shake our heads when we watch the city and the county bicker—again—about police protection, when we see police cars painted yet another color.

Come on, people! Get it together.

How many meetings/studies/rallies/powwows/questionnaires/ workshops/to-dos/accidents/letters to the editor/guest columns/ appearances before City Council does it take to get a third (!) (OK, maybe it's a fourth) bike lane? Did the world come to an end when Price Street became one way with a bike lane?

When's the last time you heard anyone mention the opioid crisis? Yes, it's a beautiful afternoon—the dogwoods!—but every day more than 115 Americans overdose and die. Surely a few of those are unfortunate souls in Savannah. We know the emergency rooms are filled. We know a for-profit hospital has replaced Memorial Health University Medical Center. We know how hard it is to get insurance. But who is being proactive about these things? Who is even talking about them? How many stories do we have to read—how many people do we have to feed (at least a couple hundred a day at last check)—about the homeless population, many of whom are veterans? We need housing for this population. How many fundraisers do we have to attend for a project that has been ignored by local government?

"Who would you say are Savannah's change agents?" one of my friends asked, using a fancy phrase for people who work to transform a community.

I named a few, but then I was stuck. I couldn't answer. We have enthusiastic newcomers, a dyed-in-the-wool Irish population, a bunch of stellar teachers fighting the good fight, some out-of-the-box artists.

We have an enviable growing season, several historic neighborhoods, a nearby ocean, plenty of high-end restaurants.

We also have a stuck-in-the-mud Chamber of Commerce with the "same-old, same-old way of doing things" mentality.

I love you, Savannah, but I don't always like you. Somehow, we have got to enjoy the weather and move the dial. But oh, how I long for those halcyon honeymoon days.

3/10/18

WORDS TO SANDY WEST ON HER 99TH BIRTHDAY
FROM SOME OF HER FRIENDS

To celebrate your 99th birthday, I am:

Calling my mom, even though it isn't Sunday
Taking an extra-long walk with my six kids—
     four dogs and two cats
Adopting a baby loggerhead sea turtle named Karen who was
     found on Jekyll Island
Enjoying a second helping of dessert
Singing out loud and strong at the Merle Haggard concert
Making a Sandy hand puppet for you to wear on your left hand
     *s*o that, when you have one of those worrisome things
     that you can't do anything about, you can look at the
     puppet and have a conversation with yourself and let
     the worry go out into the Ossabaw forest
Reading a story to my baby in the womb

AGE AND TIME

1 / *It starts with an S (Or is it an N?)*

You're at an art opening. The place is jammed. It's festive. A woman comes up and starts talking to you. You like her; you know that. You know her; you're sure of that, too. You pick up a conversation you had the last time you saw her. It's a good conversation, something about dogs, old dogs. Or maybe it was about the artist, the one from Pickens County. A librarian. But you can't focus. Your mind leaps ahead. You hope and pray your friend, who is off getting you a drink, doesn't come up right then because you can't quite remember the name of the person in front of you and then how would you introduce her?

You're saved before your friend returns. Either the conversation trails off or the other person sees someone she knows and moves on. You do too, but with urgency, when you see an ally whose name you do know. "Quick, that woman over there, the one in the short red dress, the one I was just talking to. What's her name?" If you're lucky she'll put you out of your misery. You'll be saved. For now. But will you remember it later?

"It starts with an S," you say, trying not to panic but anxious to know, right then, the name of that woman in the short red dress. "One syllable. We met her at so-and-so's party. Remember? A birthday party, great food."

Your ally stares back. Then, with a certain amount of sarcasm, maybe a little snark, she repeats your phrase. "'So-and-so?' Can you be a little more specific?"

"You know," you babble forth, still hopeful you'll get to the promised land. "The one who was married to what's-his-name, so-and-so's brother from Atlanta."

"Oh wait. The one who moved to Mexico for health insurance?"

"The brother?"

"No! The one who was married. Remember? One of her eyes drifted. You never knew which one to look at. I think she had a glass eye from when her brother poked her with a stick when they were kids."

"That was someone else," you answer. "Her brother didn't poke her. She ran into a branch. She reminds me of my cousin's ex-sister-in-law."

"The cousin from Detroit who moved to California?"

"Not that one. The one who still lives there, married to my lawyer cousin, Steve."

"Stevie?"

"Now he's Steve. Maybe you met him as Stevie."

"OK, let's focus. Can you give me more than 'so-and-so' and 'what's-his-name?' Where does she live? How old is she?"

"I don't know. Who can tell about age? I see her all the time and can never remember her name. The last time I saw her she was with you-know-who at whatchamacallit's house."

"The one who lived down the street in Doug's old house and re-married her first husband?"

"Bingo. Yes. Doug had already moved out, two people back. The one who went to SCAD before she dropped out and left town in the middle of the night."

"She didn't drop out. She got really sick, remember?"

"Hold on! Did she die or did I just dream that?"

"That's terrible. She didn't die. She just got the heck out of town. I don't think the marriage thing was working out."

"Well, she did get really sick."

"Yeah, but that's not the same as dying."

"I'll give you that. Anyway, it's not that important."

"Wait! It's not an S. Did I say S? I think it's a C."

"Let's go through the alphabet."

11/17/19

2 / Birthday thoughts
(Don't forget
to wear lipstick)

The question is inevitable: So, what'd you do on your birthday?
Buried a chicken, I started, caught up with the concrete finisher, picked
some peas, bought yet another capacitor trying to extend the life of an
aging air-conditioning unit, planted some basil, cropped the last of the
collards, made a train reservation to go see the Tampa Bay Rays (not
the Devil Rays, not anymore) in St. Petersburg, Florida, tried to avoid
a dive-bombing mockingbird feeding her chicks high in my lime tree,
paid a late bill, ate some rice cakes in the morning, a piece of ricotta
almond cake in the evening.

You know, the usual things.

Then, out of the blue, I teared up. I recalled the first time my
mother forgot my birthday. For the longest time, there were the calls
and the cards. And then they stopped. It shouldn't have been a surprise. During my visits, I'd push her around the building in her wheel-
chair. We'd watch the robins and sing what I called the "Robin Song",
popular in 1926. "When the red, red robin comes bob, bob, bobbin'
along." We'd play Bingo (sort of) and eat ice cream. Once, when I
tucked her into bed at 6:30, she said, "This was the best day of my life.
If only Jane were here."

Was that really in this same lifetime?

Like the month, my mother, born on March 1, came in like a lion
and went out like a lamb. Maybe it was the Lexapro. Maybe she decided to trick us and go all zen in the end. Maybe she wanted us to

know the fretting just wasn't worth it. If so, her timing was good. If she had to listen to the 24/7 news today, she'd be apoplectic. If she knew the "Made in America" sticker meant the washing machine was assembled in America while the parts were made in China, well, she'd blow a gasket.

On her birthday, she'd go to Jack's for the promised free car wash and Bill Knapp's, a small chain of family restaurants in the Midwest that would discount your meal by your age. "But what if I live to 102?" she once asked. "Does that mean I would get some money back?"

When I found out recently I won some kind of state column-writing award, I couldn't wait to tell my nephew, not for a pat on the back but for old time's sake. We both knew what my mother would have said: "Do you get any money for that? Do you get a raise?"

I miss her loopy handwriting, her letters, her reminders. Be nice. Mind your Ps and Qs. Write Nana. Don't forget to wear lipstick. P.S.: It wouldn't hurt to dust your house once in a while. Here's $20: Buy yourself a new outfit.

I don't have to miss her slightly crooked feet. I have them.

Of all the stuff I cleared out of her house—the scarves, the hosiery, the garters (!), the socks, the swimming goggles, the costume jewelry, the beads—one of the only things I decided to keep was a tin of her eyeglasses. They span the decades. They're square, round, rectangular, thick, thin, tinted with cat eyes, decorated with rhinestones. I remember each pair, maybe because I see them on her in her half-dozen passport photos, which I also kept. But why did she keep them? And what am I supposed to do with them or with those letters?

I have started using her silverware, the good stuff, the kind you used to put away for company, except it always needed polishing so you didn't bother, except now it doesn't need polishing because it's getting used, every day, in every way. What took me so long? I have one plate left of my grandmother's pattern. I think of her every time I use it, which is good because I don't remember going to her funeral. Or my grandfather's. And I loved these people. I never got a straight answer out of my mother about that. Something about not wanting to bother me. That's so baffling. Just one more baffling thing about families.

So many questions. So many birthdays. Bring 'em on.

5/12/18

3 / At the Three-quarter mark (Portobello: you know, "that city in Portugal")

It's not easy being seventy-five. There's a lot to live up to. At fifty- or sixty-five, you have an excuse. You're still working on stuff. You're still polishing your game, getting it all together. With a little push, a little practice, you could still get better. But with three-quarters of a century down the hatch, you're starting to run out of time. Your fingers aren't as nimble. Neither are your feet. Ten years ago, when I participated in the U.S. Masters Swimming program, diving into the pool at 5 a.m. three days a week, the coach filmed us underwater and offered critiques. "See," he said, after I thought I did a pretty good job on the butterfly stroke. "It's your feet. They're never going to be flexible enough to really propel you." Thanks a lot, coach.

Then there was the woman thirty years my junior. When told it was my birthday, she said, "You're closing in on it." I didn't ask her what the "it" was. I think we both knew. Me too, she said. She was turning forty. "I've got to start making my move," she mused.

Most of the time, I've noticed, people may pretend to be listening to you, but they're really thinking about themselves. It's best, I remind myself, not to expect too much. It works out better that way. But ah ... the words. They're just not as forthcoming. I'm having trouble remembering the word portobello. "You know," I almost said. "That city in Portugal."

As essayist Roger Angell once wrote: When he's in conversation with someone and, in the middle of a story, senses a blank spot coming up, he might stop and think (as I am now), "Did I tell that story or just think I told that story?" When he's relating something that happened, he might, as he put it, send a scout up ahead to corral the words for the end of the story. If he sees some of the words getting away, he (and I) might stall for time, take a detour, throw in something we are dead sure of, hoping all the while the bon mots might show themselves—or the person to whom you were speaking would interrupt with something about themselves.

At the three-quarter mark, we're starting to question ourselves, but we try not to talk about it too much. Now, with the least little muscle spasm or twitch you panic, especially if it happens in the middle of the night. The knee: Did it always feel this way? The back: Should I be worried? Maybe it was just from weeding. But maybe it's something more serious. How many pain-killing pills is it safe to take anyway?

"Why does that hurt?" you ask Dr. John, the chiropractor.

"You're not going to like my answer," he says.

"OK. Tell me."

"It's because you're old."

"Older," I say.

"OK, older."

Still. I could worry. I don't like that number. I liked seventy-four better. Or seventy-three. But seventy-five? Smack in the middle of the seventies. Who could possibly be this old? Gloria Steinem, for one. She's eighty-one. She said sixty was great. It was beyond what she called the "feminine prison." I think she meant you could be your own self. But eighty—well, eighty is about mortality. I don't like that word. The whole thing makes me a little nervous. But as Ms. Steinem said, it's a little freeing, too. Free to do what I want, and when. Free to wear those comfortable shirts with frayed collars, loose pants at any time, comfortable shoes. Free to use the words "moron" or "idiot" when I think they apply, which seems to be more and more. Free of vanity. I never used to like the circles around my eyes from swimming goggles. Then my cousin Andy, a big swimmer, said, "Fish face, wear it with pride." It's a special club we belong to. We love other people in this club.

We are not afraid to say anything foolish. Sarcasm takes over. "I think you're in the wrong building," a woman told me today when we saw one another at Savannah's Cathedral Basilica of St. John the Baptist, on Abercorn Street. I was at a baptism—the first one I've ever been to in my whole life. Plenty of brises, bat mitzvahs, bar mitzvahs and burials. No baptisms. I had cooked Israeli fries with this woman at the annual Jewish Food Festival, a major fundraiser for Congregation Mickve Israel.

"Your building is a few blocks over," she said, referring to Mickve Israel. We laughed. At age seventy-five, I wish religion didn't segregate people so much. That's stupid. I wish skin color didn't matter. It's only skin color! Seeing that as a meaningful difference is idiotic. I wish the government paid as much attention to people as they do to buildings. That's a no-brainer. I wish we had more music in the parks. That would be so easy. I wish I could have been in the audience a few weeks ago when African-American billionaire Robert F. Smith told the Class of 2019 Morehouse University graduates he was paying off their student loans. He believes in paying it forward. I like that.

5/5/19

4 / Cousins: the key
to family mysteries
(Who else knew your parents?)

In some families—not all—cousins don't mean that much when you're young. They're just people close to your own age, people you're supposed to like, who also call your grandparents Nana and Papa. If cousins are a year or two older (or younger), well, who cares about them? He's such a baby. She's only in third grade. Such a huge difference to a kid. If they live in another town, another state, they might as well be strangers.

Except they're not. They're your cousins. They're blood. They know things no one else does. They remember things. And now that the world is so much more connected, they can get your number and call you out of the blue.

"Hey, Jane, this is your cousin Bert," the message began a few days ago. "I got a question for you."

Bert, as in Aunt Joan's son? The one we called Rusty because he had red hair? Could it be? It's only been about five decades. I called him back right away. He got right to the point.

"Remember that black-and-white photograph Uncle Harry and Aunt Trudy took that one Thanksgiving Day in Huntington Woods when we were all there, the one that hung in Papa's den all those years?"

The one I snagged, I thought, and held onto through at least twenty different addresses in five different states? Yep. I remember that one, I said. I'm looking at it right now. I love it. There you are in a red plaid vest, to go with your hair, I assume. I remember that vest. You were—what, twelve?

I had totally forgotten it was taken on Thanksgiving. That's what made Rusty think about calling me, I guess. Holidays will do that. Even before he asked, I said I'd be happy to make him a print.

"But can I still call you Rusty?" I said.

I know nothing about him now, who he votes for, what movies he prefers, what he likes to do on Sunday afternoons, if he plants garlic or likes to cook collards. I only know we played together. We shared grandparents. We knew where they hid the good candy, how they snored at night, how much they loved to watch "I Love Lucy." He probably remembers the thick orthopedic shoes our grandfather wore, how our grandmother was always going to doctors, the contraption she set up to make chopped liver in that sunny back kitchen of their ranch house on Ludlow Avenue in Huntington Woods, Michigan.

For the first three or four decades of our lives, none of this seemed very important or relevant. Why would it? You take it for granted. When one of your cousins invites you to a birthday party with people you don't know, you whine, "Mom, do I have to go?" They are not your best friends. Not even the death of a grandparent—which can happen when you are living out of town or when you're busy with a different life—brings you closer together. Much of the time you tend to be closer to one set of grandparents than another. This has more to do with your parents than with you. The whys of these relationships often go to the grave. Why did our nuclear unit "go with" the Modell side and not the Fishman side? We don't know. Rusty was a Modell cousin. Every time we get together, we Fishman cousins, we ponder this but we don't get very far. No one is around who can give us answers.

When I visit a cousin who lives in Minneapolis, she tells me, "You're a Fishman. You have a big head. You're not very mechanical." You're right. I do and I'm not.

It's only when one or both of your parents pass on that cousins start to become more important or more interesting. Or when one of them remembers a certain photograph. Then a certain pride kicks in at the descriptor. "This is my cousin Nancy," I say when Nancy and her husband Ronnie visit. Or Marsha. Or Bonnie. Or Maggie, Andy,

Carol, Beth or Steve (who used to be Stevie). As a kid I always felt I had so many cousins, but I really didn't.

When I go to a restaurant with my cousins Melvin and Karla and the maître d' might say, "Fishman party of four," I do a double take and think: There are four of us? Then I remember. I'm not the only one with that name. Melvin is a second cousin. Our fathers were first cousins. That kind of thing used to mean something. Now it doesn't. Melvin and my other cousins know things about my parents and our family I don't know or don't remember. Some of it seems silly to me. You wanted my father to be your father? Really? Because my father would play catch with you and your father wouldn't?

We have so much in common genetically but we all turn out so differently. It's no accident that we make up our own family as we go along, that we gather our own sisters and brothers, people who are closer to us emotionally.

I'm still hoping a cousin or two will say something that will unlock the mystery that is family. But in the meantime they are my cugina and cugino. And one of them I still call Rusty.

11/17/16

5 / *It's hip to be gray (Me and Richard Gere)*

Gray hair is trending. I read this somewhere. I can't tell you where. I can't even tell you what "trending" means. All I think when I hear that term is, "Someone is using 'trend' as a gerund? Really?" But I think it's a good thing for people such as myself who are walking around with gray hair. Translated, it means we are trending. We are happening. We are wearing our hair as a sign of something. This is assuming the declarations of young people are important because those are the people who are doing the "trending." Or so I read. They, the youngsters, want the silver vixen look. And they are paying good money for it. Can you imagine?

On the other hand, I have loved watching Toni Morrison's hair pick up a little gray dusting year by year—the same with Alice Walker—although mostly I couldn't give two figs for the color of their hair: black, white, red, purple. It's their writing I like, their thinking. They challenge us.

The rest of us have to make do with humor, with boldness. The other day, I was crossing Park Avenue, coming out of Brighter Day Natural Foods Market, just kind of barging out into the street because that's what trendsetting, impatient people with gray hair do. We step out. We don't wait for permission. It's kind of a crazy corner over by the Forsyth Park tennis courts, but when the driver in the Honda Fit saw me and let me walk across, I turned to the woman who was also crossing and said, "It's because of my gray hair." She answered, "You think?" That's when I broke the news to her. "Gray hair is trending." You've heard the expression "Black don't crack"? As in the skin of African Americans? It's smooth and youthful and beautiful and rarely marred by wrinkles. Well, the new expression is "Gray hair don't care."

The new movement is called the granny hair trend. It's edgy. And people are paying good money to get their hair to look that way.

Of course Richard Gere, who is trending 66, came by his gray hair naturally. To his credit, he didn't change it. Then again he was once married to supermodel Cindy Crawford and he's a Buddhist. He's got self-confidence. The same with Anderson Cooper. No one ever complained about his hair. No matter that Cooper is related to the Vanderbilts and looks like he's 12. Then there's John Travolta, who wears a very bad rug. I'm pretty sure bad rugs are trending as much or as little as Scientology.

I know that time flies, but I do recall a heated debate over putting a woman on the airwaves as an anchor during the prime time 6 p.m. newscast. That was a gender thing, not an age thing. The horror! The public won't take a woman's voice seriously, the argument went. Women don't have enough gravitas, no matter how dark or gray their hair is. There's no telling how many women could have done a better job than Brian Williams, who despite his good (blond) hair had a little trouble with the truth and with going after the news. But somehow it didn't matter. Good hair and male genes translate into big bucks and lots of airtime.

Now I'm more concerned with the spelling of the word. Turns out *gray* (with an A) is the preferred spelling in the States and *grey* (with an E) is what the Brits do—unless it's a dog you're talking about (greyhound) or a restaurant (Savannah's The Grey). Then it's an E.

Anyway, I'm over the color. I've made my peace with gray. I'm waiting to see what these trendsetting "fifty shades of grey" "women will do next to add a little gravitas or dignity to their looks. I myself can't wait for the sleepy, droopy-eyelid look to hit the big time. You know, the hooded eyelids of Lauren Bacall when she is talking to that tough guy, private eye Philip Marlowe (Humphrey Bogart) in *The Big Sleep*? Does anyone have any word on this?

4/12/15

6 / Do I sound old?
(John-John
and Janis Joplin)

For a while the question was—and still might be, for those who haven't given up trying (and who still care)—"Do I look fat?" (For them there's always blousy, oversized clothing, mostly black, large scarves and mirrors that stop at the waist).

Then there's the memorable selfie of someone posed in front of a high-rise or teetering on high heels (or, for men, shoes with lifts) asking: "Does this make me look tall?"

But mostly these days, the most-feared question one may think, but rarely verbalize, is: "Do I sound old?"

Oh, what the heck. Old is old, no matter how much you dye your hair (there are always those weeks when you're behind schedule and those gray roots show through), no matter how subtly you scoot closer to someone so you can cup your ear to hear better or how you hide your mouth so you can floss that strand of lettuce caught between implants. (When did we floss so much?)

You're in the middle of a perfectly natural activity with people, people of all generations, everyone doing the same thing, and somehow age comes up.

It could be in relation to your first concert (a tired and overworked question; OK, for the hundredth time, it was Janis Joplin), where you were when President Kennedy was shot (or his son, John-John—another giveaway for one's age, by the way, recalling someone whose good looks, brains and challenging legacy landed him many, many bold-faced mentions in gossip columns—died in a plane accident), your first (gigantic, probably desktop) computer, your struggles with the correction fluid known as Wite-Out, your experiences with Fred Rogers, aka Mister Rogers, or the speaker at your college graduation (raise your hand if you've heard of economist and Harvard intellectual John Kenneth Galbraith. He spoke at my sweltering May afternoon 1966 graduation from the University of Michigan, where I was one of thousands to get a degree, a good portion of them English majors. Remember English majors? It wasn't the best major, in retrospect).

Right about then is when you step in to put people out of their misery. You do the math for them.

"Yes, that's right. I'm ..." Fill in the blank. The age changes depending on what year the subject comes up.

P.S.: I don't hear too many people listening to podcasts or recorded lectures of Galbraith's works. They're trying to find the latest humorist, memoirist or comic. They're trying to stay ahead of the curve. I thought of that question — "Do I sound old?" — the other night when my friend Lesley and I popped into a bar after a movie. We had just seen "Eighth Grade." Lord have mercy. That movie is guaranteed to take you back to those uncomfortable middle-school years of feeling left out, of caring too much what other people think of you without knowing who "you" are, of trying to fit what seems like a square peg into a round hole. Troubling times, and all before knowing it's cool to be uncool.

If we thought life was hard then, think of what it's like now for kids growing up in the age of social media, when the term "like" takes on a whole new meaning. Warning: The film is suspenseful. The good thing is the presence of things like Snapchat and Instagram. (I guess.) They offer the misfit kids a creative outlet to express their misery, should they choose to use it.

The movie was provocative. There was a lot to digest.

Lesley and I decided to go out, have a drink or two, and talk about it. Long ago, there might have been a time when a crowded, noisy room with deafening music and jockeying elbows near the bar was attractive. Not so now.

We walked in, found a table, ordered some drinks and tried to talk. But first I asked the server for a napkin because I was taught it's not good to place a perspiring drink on wood. I tried to be polite and frame the question without any attitude, without sounding as if I were old and she were young ("Did that sound old?" I asked my friend) without even knowing what that meant, except if the kids in "Eighth Grade" didn't want to do anything to stand out and make people stare at them, I didn't either. I did not want to do anything that would make me look old. I had already asked for a slice of lime and a glass of water, trying very hard not to sound arch or snippy.

So far, so good. Except we had sat down next to a table of six loud people high-fiving and pouring straight from a bottle. Hey, it was Friday night. They were already well into their cups. Early on, I knew we had made a mistake. We should have picked up our drinks and moved to another table. They were there first. They were not going to move or lower their voices.

We had no options.

We tried to ignore them and huddle closer to talk.

Then it was time to go home. I tried to tip generously. I hoped we could get out of there without any glares or stares. It wasn't easy. We don't hold back. We're people who are old, hoping we are people who don't sound old.

8/11/18

7 / Otoliths:
they're not Russian
(Lovely word: benign)

"Props," said the young pharmacist on DeRenne Avenue who could not have been older than twelve as she started to wrap up the cuff, the monitor, the squeeze ball after she gave me my blood pressure numbers.

She didn't look concerned so I had to ask, "Props. Is that a good thing?"

"It's good," she said. "You know, like short for respect, proper respect. Your numbers look good." And then she was back at her post behind the counter.

"But wait. Do you think we should take it again?" I asked. "Just to be sure."

"Nope," she said with certainty, with pride. "I don't let anyone else use this equipment. It's mine. It's accurate."

Well, OK then, Ms. Pharmacist-At-Your-Corner-drugstore. Props. And thanks for being there when I needed you. I'm serious. Much easier than going to the emergency room.

Time for a Dilly Bar.

But what about the dizziness? Do I get props for that? She didn't know, but she was quite certain I wasn't going to have a stroke right then and there, that I would live to see another day, to pull another weed, to read another chapter in Thomas Wolfe's *Look Homeward, Angel*. Which was good. The book is a tome. Which meant I could ignore the dizziness for yet another day. Which is how I like to treat anomalies. Ignore them and they will go away.

I know about dizziness—like when you are foolish enough to go on a roller-coaster, which I no longer do. I know about dizziness from walking up and down a train car, too. Which I do with care (if not grace), bouncing from one seat to another to another, like a pinball game where the moving thingy pings off cushion after cushion, for which you get points. Or props.

But this lightheadedness was different. This was a little scarier. It happened a little more often, especially when it involved getting up from bed in the middle of the night, from a chair in the afternoon, or from a yoga mat after performing a downward dog. The room, previously still and very much anchored, would spin. The ceiling, too. Round and round she goes. There was no roller-coaster to blame it on this time; no train, either. That's when I hustled to the drugstore for the blood pressure check. That's when I went to see the doctor. He didn't seem worried.

"This happens in old people," he said.

"Older," I corrected him.

"Older," he said, to appease me. Then he had a diagnosis: "BPV, benign positional vertigo. I'm probably 95 percent certain."

I liked the word "benign." I loved the word "benign." I asked him to repeat it. Then I asked him to write it down. He placated me. Again. It's when stuff gets stuck in your middle ear, he said, although I'm sure he didn't use the words "stuff" and "stuck". When doctors mumble that language, it's so hard to follow. This vertigo thing starts when free-floating pieces of calcium lodge in a little ear canal and start to interfere with your balance, he said. Kind of like free-floating anxiety, I thought. He sent me for a test to confirm his theory, then to see a physical therapist. Oh, and he said I should use hydrogen peroxide.

Hydrogen peroxide? I said. That's so retro. I liked that.

The test that hooked me up to the computer and measured my eye movement took 10 minutes. I looked at a red dot on the wall and turned my head one way, then the other, faster and faster. What's this for? I asked the technician. To see if you're dizzy, she said. I already know I'm dizzy, I answered.

Next step. The physical therapist. You lie down, turn your head quickly one way, then the other. Something like that. It's called the Epley maneuver. I was following directions, not memorizing the movements. The therapist looked deeply into my eyes and told me to repeat the maneuver. Bingo. No dizziness. You're cured, he said in so many words. I liked those words, too. Come back if it happens again. Again, so retro. They just had to jiggle the calcium pieces.

Still on the medical appointment treadmill, I was sent to see someone else to get the results from the test. That's when I learned about otoliths. Sounds very Russian, I said to the doctor. Very timely, wouldn't you say? Oligarch, KGB, USSR. No comment. Your otoliths have fallen out of alignment, he announced. Otoliths are calcium particles, kind of like little beads that balance on your finger. When they fall out of position, you lose your balance. Wikipedia says that counting the annual growth rings on the otoliths is a common technique for estimating the age of fish. What? First, a Russian conspiracy. Then a fish story. There's a reason I'm not a medical person.

If it happens again, I should lie down, assume a fetal position and thrust my head rapidly in the other direction. The doctor in a purple shirt plopped down on the examining table and demonstrated. Then he got up, made some notes and said, "It's been a pleasure."

I returned the compliment. "Props." By then he was out the room and on to the next patient.

7/22/17

8 / *The longest day of the year with a book (Who can resist that?)*

I almost finished, but I stopped. Deep into a really great book, *Little Bee* by Chris Cleave, I decided to save the last one-third for an early evening read at Tybee Island, where I planned to draw my plastic beach chair close to the water, pull my hat down low and let the sound of the tide and the wind block out all other distractions.

It took a little while to get everything organized. But it was June 21, the longest day of the year, the summer solstice, so there was no hurry to pack the car and leave the house in the city, no hurry to get back to my book, which I could have finished the previous night but chose, instead, to close so I could have it to look forward to the next day.

The unread book would be a little secret I could carry around all day, because I knew I was in the middle of a great story that would not disappoint. I could save the end because I knew the next day was the longest day of the year. I wanted it to be memorable, not that any day would beat the time I boarded a train, the Silver Meteor, in New York City at 7 a.m., unaware of the significance (or the length, some ten hours of light) of the day, heading back for Savannah with a book in hand, Michael Cunningham's *The Hours*.

On this trip, another summer solstice, I would arrive in Savannah around 9:30 at night, with just the slightest sliver of daylight in the western sky, but not before looking out the window of the train and thinking (in all caps, I am sure), IS THIS DAY EVER GOING TO END? AM I EVER GOING TO BE ABLE TO GET OFF THIS TRAIN?

At home, before heading to Tybee, I was patient in my preparations, a far cry from my usual behavior, which more closely resembles: Let's go! Hurry up! Come on!

At the last minute, I succumbed to habit and took my phone, but I turned it off.

I remembered to pocket the requisite number of quarters (fifteen minutes per quarter at the parking meter), took my time getting gas, crested the Bull River Bridge, watched my speed, and eased into a legal parking spot on one of the numbered streets off Butler Avenue. Once set up on the sand, I glanced at my book but didn't open it right away. Feeling the righteous hunger of the beach, I dipped into dinner, some leftover tabouli from a high school graduation party I had attended a few days earlier.

I watched the parade of campers from The Fresh Air Home Camp, one line of girls in pink, another of boys in blue. I dug my toes deep into the sand and followed a kite.

I pretended I was on vacation on Cape Cod, somewhere I have never been. I leaned back and forgot about everything but the sand, the water, the breeze.

It was so windy that I drew a towel over my bent and very white legs. I wondered if I would even get into the water, it was that much cooler than in town.

I swore I would go to Tybee every day for the rest of the summer. The beach will do that to you.

And then, with all the time in the world, on the longest day of the year, I reached for my glasses and opened my book, an unsettling Ian McEwen-like tale about two women — an immigrant girl from Nigeria and a middle-class journalist from London — who share a disturbing experience on a beach, not unlike the one I was enjoying at the moment, except there were no soldiers carrying rifles on my beach and it was not the solstice on their beach.

Cleave, the author, is a columnist for *The Guardian* newspaper in London.

It's one of those books I knew nothing about, except the person who recommended it, which, in most cases, is good enough for me. I read for the next two hours, savoring each page until I flipped ahead and realized I had only four more pages to go. Now that's a good book, I thought, when you are that far into the story and you still don't know how it's going to end.

And that's when the words started to blur. I squinted. I narrowed my eyes. I shifted my chair and brought the book closer to my face. Then I looked around and saw why. The longest day of the year had run out of daylight. It was getting too dark to read. The moon, five days short of being full, was not quite bright enough.

I had one paragraph to go, then one sentence until I would know what happened to Little Bee. I was desperate. I had run out of time. I had no choice. I searched in my beach bag, found my phone, pushed the "on" button and got just enough light to finish the book.

By then the longest day of the year was over.

6/26/10

9 / *Who can keep up?*
(The phone knows it all)

Last week, without hesitation or doubt, I dated a check 2005.

"That's nothing," a woman said when I told her this story. "The other day, I wrote my maiden name on a check. I've been married 15 years."

Who can keep up?

Some friends are visiting this week from Durham, North Carolina. I was sure it had been less than four or five months since we had last seen one another.

"Nope," said Gene. "It was on my birthday."

That never changes. It was the end of August.

Busted.

Sometimes it works in our favor, this memory thing. Was it my left knee I broke last summer in Tel Aviv, or the right? Or is that just reinventing the past to keep from going crazy with the truth? Now I hear myself speaking of the month-long stay-at-home knee recovery period in almost glowing terms. "It wasn't so bad. I read three books. I got to experience stillness."

One thing's for sure: It's hard to remember pain. When I tell people my knee hurt so much trying to navigate the quarter-inch threshold between the bedroom and the bathroom that I had to literally pick up my leg, it's the truth. Not that I feel the pain. I don't anymore. That ability to block out or forget the pain is, I'm pretty certain, a good thing, although I've always found that disappointments carry a greater level of emotion than achievements, like submitting work to a writing contest and not winning anything—boo, hiss, rats—versus taking first, second or third place (of course who wants to come in second, which is so close to first? Third is better than second). But the award? Whew, OK, I won. That's good. All with little or no emotion.

Other things are certain, too: war, homicide, suicide bombers, crooked politicians, decaying infrastructure, more bluster, more air strikes, more collateral damage. If you smudge out the date on today's news, you might just as well be reading yesterday's news—and not just news from 2015. Nothing new about regime change. Iran, Chile, Guatemala, Iraq, Afghanistan. Doesn't work. Nations, like people, have to change themselves.

It's a wonder we read anything at all in the news. Some people don't. Some people on the drive to and from work listen to Mahler or Mendelssohn or Nine Inch Nails. News updates? Paris bombings? What Paris bombings? Didn't those happen last year? As far as I can see, these people don't seem to be missing out on anything.

I tried that one day. I left my phone at home (ok, not deliberately), but with it all vital information, camera, calendar, calculator, date, weather, connection to news updates, reminders, email and "notes". I swear, my shoulders dropped three inches. I stood taller. I sat and watched a hawk on my neighbor's chimney (he was sitting very still, just waiting for me to open the chicken coop and let the girls out for some exercise, some worms). My arms swung a bit freer. My mind, well, it was just a little freer, too.

It didn't last. I'm an addict. If it weren't so serious, if so many people didn't keep dying, I might regard the news as I do a television series. As it is, I might as well just watch *Homeland* and get lost in the wily, worried eyes of Claire Danes aka Carrie Mathison (at least we know she won't die; she can't, since she's the main character) or Mandy Patinkin as Saul Berenson (he can't die either; he's another star and he's the former head of the CIA; they don't die, right?). At least we get to see what Berlin looks like.

At least, on Thanksgiving, we get to eat good, laugh good, be around good friends and feel good. That never changes, except when it does, like in 2020.

I was talking to someone the other day when, out of the blue, he

Who can keep up?

asked how long I have known a mutual friend.

"Since 1989," I said to Ben. "You probably weren't even born yet."

"I was 2," he answered.

A few minutes later, he asked me over to dinner. What's a few years, anyway? I thought. Nothing. Nothing at all. It's just time.

11/29/15

10 / *Alexa,*
when will I die?
(Just kidding)

"Nice to see you again," she said, moving in for a quick kiss on the cheek. "Don't get too close to me. I'm on the verge."

Everyone, or so it seems, is on the verge. It's the season, teetering between wellness and sickness, happiness and despair. Still we forge on. We can beat this. We slice one more piece of cheese. We dive into the dip, drenching the saltine. We try Aaron's mother's homemade chocolate turtles. We hold the bottle of Betsy's eggnog—the real stuff —upside down, going for the last drop, dammit. We eat cookies the children made—"the children made them!"—even though we didn't want to, even though they are pure sugar.

The rain, in December, won't let up.

We take a walk on the wild side and plunge some homemade biscotti, designed to destroy a tooth, into a cup of coffee. For breakfast, we sit down to hollandaise-drenched Oysters Rockefeller that Travis has generously made with last night's leftover oysters.

Just one more piece of Enstrom chocolate-covered, almond-filled toffee, OK? For breakfast. C'mon. Enstrom is a family business. It goes back to 1919. How bad could that little piece be? Anyway, your darling cousins sent them. Just one more piece.

No sugar, the acupuncturist says when you limp in for a session because you are on the verge. You are on the brink and you don't want to be. You want joy. It's your spleen, the acupuncturist says. No alcohol. No wine.

No wonder our dreams are all over the place. We've lost our rhythm. Our cadence is off. We have no flow.

"You already had your Christmas, right?" someone will say, referring to Chanukah, a holiday of miracles that has nothing to do with Christmas except maybe the proximity of the occasion.

You go to the movies because it's the holidays and you want a little distraction. It works, somewhat. You cry at *A Star Is Born*. You shake your head at the weirdness of *The Favourite*. But when you leave *Vice*—the biopic of Dick Cheney—you're off-kilter. You're on the verge, again, this time from fury, from wrath. All the memories of the prevaricating '90s are dredged up again, just when you think you have seen it all, that nothing could be as bad as today's version of leadership. It's scary how fast we forget, how much we forget. How could we have let that happen? What do you say now, Colin Powell? Are you on the verge?

Did I really need to see that?

"Who's Dick Cheney?" This, from someone born in the late '90s, bless her heart. What are weapons of mass destruction? How could he be worse than what's-his-name?

Did you have a nice Christmas?

We awake to rain. More rain.

The best present someone else got? A cheerful red, green and white sweatshirt that reads, "Oy to the world." (Now why didn't I think of that?)

The most politically correct holiday message? A video of a home-schooled, gender-schooled seven-year-old working on a gingerbread house complete with a "snow person." (I know, I know, don't start up with me.)

The best present I got—although nineteen years into the century, I'm still trying to figure out or come to terms with certain things—was one of those voice-controlled robots that plays any music you want (as long as you get her name right; she is Alexa, not Alexis, which is what I tried the first five times).

Alexa, I say from a prone position on the couch because, well, I'm on the verge and at the moment that's the best I can do. Play Marianne Faithfull's "The Gypsy Faerie Queen." Play Nina Simone. Let me hear that beautiful, mournful, soulful voice that's seen it all, felt it all, lived it all, echo through the house, sounding better than any speakers I've ever had. And I've had a lot. And because that's the way life is, all of this happens the same day the needle on my sweet little analog-ish record player goes belly up. It's that darn needle. The new one just won't slip in.

It doesn't feel right not to say thank you to Alexa.

Who needs to leave home?

Except none of this robot-responding, Big Brother thing seems right. What's next? Alexa, what's my name? When will I die? How will I die?

Here we are: 2019. Nearly a fifth of the way through the century but after six days in the new year, we're no longer on the verge. Maybe on the brink, but not the verge.

Happy New Year, my friends. We'll get through this, right?

1/5/19

JANE FISHMAN is the author of five earlier books;
*So What's the Hurry? Tales From the Train, I Grew it My
Way: How Not to Garden, The Woman Who Saved an
Island: Sandy West and Ossabaw Island, The Dirt on Jane:
an Anti-Memoir,* and *Everyone's Gotta Be Somewhere.*
She lives in Savannah.

Made in the USA
Columbia, SC
30 July 2021